Racism's impact on Black nursing.

Margarita G. Grant

Abstract

This qualitative phenomenological research study explored nursing educators' meanings of the phenomenon of racism and their perceptions of the effects of racism on Black nursing students at Predominately White Institutions (PWIs). In an online qualitative survey and individual interviews, faculty, staff, and administrators of PWI nursing programs discussed meanings of racism, their understanding of the obstacles Black nursing students face at PWIs, and support systems in place for Black students in their nursing programs. The researcher selected Critical Race Theory (CRT) as the theoretical framework for this study, with an understanding that Black students are often faced with greater challenges to completing nursing programs than their White counterparts. The attrition rate is higher among Black nursing students at PWIs than it is for other students (Eudy & Brooks, 2022) and Black students experience racism more often than students of other races (Ackerman-Barger et al., 2020; Hall & Fields, 2012). Findings from this study indicate that there is an awareness among educators of the effects of racism on Black nursing students. However, poor communication and lack of personal accountability for supporting Black students prevent many nursing educators at PWIs from providing tangible, realistic help to their students. Recommendations for future practice coming out of this study suggest that nursing program administrators lead the charge in demonstrating a commitment to equity and inclusion by encouraging increased communication among nursing educators and students, and by adopting practices that are more considerate and inclusive of Black nursing students.

Keywords: nursing education, faculty, staff, administrators, racism, Black students, Critical Race Theory, Predominately White Institution (PWI), awareness, support systems

Table of Contents

List of Tables

List of Figures

Chapter I. Statement of the Problem

The nursing profession has a problem. There are not enough nurses to care for a growing U.S. population that has become very racially and ethnically diverse (Green, 2020). The shortage of nurses has been exacerbated in recent years by the anticipated retirement of seasoned nurses and by masses of newer nurses exiting the profession during a global pandemic (Caravelis et al., 2023; Lopez et al., 2022; Mariani, 2022; Yordy, 2006). Producing more nurses overall, and encouraging those nurses to remain in the profession, is crucial to remedying the shortage. One approach to producing more nurses is assuring that Black nursing students and other students of color are welcomed and supported— academically and socially— in nursing school. Black students often enter nursing programs with greater challenges to completing nursing school than other students face (Eudy & Brooks, 2022). Once matriculated, students at Predominately White Institutions (PWIs) may find themselves in nursing programs where educators do not recognize the challenges of being a Black nursing student (Eudy & Brooks, 2022). Without an understanding of those challenges, nursing educators cannot address and remove the potential barriers to Black students' success at PWIs. Black students experience racism more often than students of other races (Ackerman-Barger et al., 2020; Hall & Fields, 2012). "Because of the historical vestiges of slavery, segregation, and legalized discrimination, Black people face more, and qualitatively different, discrimination and devaluation than do other POC [people of color] in the United States" (Hall & Fields, 2012, p. 27).

Some of the effects of racism on Black students' educational experiences at PWIs are mentioned briefly here and are defined and explored further in Chapter II. Review of the Literature. Black students described their experiences at PWIs as lonely, inhospitable, fueled with constant microaggressions, and riddled with stereotyping and mistrust (Ackerman-Barger &

Hummel, 2015; Ackerman-Barger et al., 2020; Attis-Josias, 2023; Bell, 2021; Childs et al., 2004; White & Fulton, 2015; White et al., 2020). Stressors for Black students at PWIs, in addition to nursing curricula centered in Whiteness, were the absence of role models of color and the lack of positive relationships with teachers (Matthews et al., 2022; White et al., 2020). Because of a multitude of stressors that may be related to race, Black students have higher rates of attrition, or non-completion of nursing school, than students from other ethnic groups (Green, 2020; Matthews et al., 2022; White et al., 2020). Attrition, microaggressions, and Whiteness are defined in the Definition of Terms section of this chapter and are discussed in detail in Chapter II. Review of the Literature.

There is insufficient documentation in nursing education literature about nursing educators at PWIs' understanding of the experience of racism in nursing education and of their understanding of the connections between racism, Black students' attrition, and the nursing shortage. The term "nursing educators" is used in this dissertation study to categorize all personnel that work with students in nursing programs. Nursing educators include faculty that teach in classroom and clinical settings, staff that work with or around students in various capacities, and administrators or leadership of nursing programs. It is unclear whether nursing educators at PWIs understand the effects of racism on Black nursing students and the challenges racism may present to successful completion of nursing school (Green, 2020). Nursing educators may not be aware of the persistent racism that pervades nursing education and negatively impacts Black nursing students (Green, 2020; White et al., 2020). Further evidence of a lack of understanding of nursing educators at PWIs about the experience of racism and the importance of addressing the challenges Black nursing students face related to racism is discussed in the literature review section of this dissertation.

Black or African American (Institute of Education Services [IES], 2023a; OMB, 1997) individuals enrolled in nursing programs in the United States, a country which has a legacy of slavery, segregation, and enduring anti-Black racism and discrimination (Hall & Fields, 2012; Iheduru-Anderson & Waite, 2022; Mitchell, 2023; White & Fulton, 2015), are considered Black nursing students in this dissertation study. Race is described by Wade et al. (2024) as an ideology "of relatively recent origin" that originated in tandem with a period of "European exploration and colonization" (Wade et al., 2024, para. 7). Race may be defined as a "social invention" used to classify people into groups based on "human differences associated with the different populations brought together in the New World" (Wade et al., 2024, para. 7). After the abolition of slavery in America, the ideology of race became further institutionalized as a system of social "division and stratification" (Wade et al., 2024, para. 7). Ethnicity "refers to a sense of identity and membership in a group that shares common language, cultural traits (values, beliefs, religion, food habits, customs, etc.), and a sense of a common history" (Wade et al., 2024, para. 12). The federal government agency, Office of Management and Budget (OMB) determines the standard language and categories used for reporting data on race and ethnicity in the U.S. The most up-to-date standards on race and ethnicity were developed in 1997 (IES, 2023a; Office of Management and Budget [OMB], 1997). The OMB standards state that race and ethnicity are to be "thought of in terms of social and cultural characteristics as well as ancestry" (OMB, 1997, p. 58782) and not as biological or genetic categories. Office of Management and Budget standards define "five minimum categories for data on race" and "two categories for data on ethnicity" (OMB, 1997, p. 58782). The categories are "Race: American Indian or Alaska Native, Asian, Black or African American, Native Hawaiian or other Pacific Islander, and White… Ethnicity: 'Hispanic or Latino' and 'Not Hispanic or Latino'" (OMB, 1997, p. 58782). Racial identification and ethnicity are still significant considerations for Americans as the population grows. It is estimated that in less than 20 years, more than half of the U.S. population will identify as a member of a racial and ethnic group other than "White" and "Not Hispanic or Latino" (Matthews et al., 2022). While the population grows, racism continues to be an issue and attributes to health inequities in the U.S. (Iheduru-Anderson & Wahi, 2022).

Racism is an organized system which involves a dominant group of people categorizing people other than themselves into social groups based on characteristics such as color. The dominant group holds power and allocates resources and opportunities based on their beliefs that people of color are inferior (Braveman et al., 2022; Iheduru-Anderson & Waite, 2022). Racism in the U.S. is founded upon a "unique and fundamental ideology about human differences" (Wade et al., 2024, para. 8) and is an enduring part of the U.S. social and legal systems (Braveman et al., 2022). Systemic racism in the U.S. seems to "reflect the natural, inevitable order of things" and is undergirded by structures such as the law, and policies and practices (Braveman et al., 2022, p. 172). The terms "systemic racism" and "structural racism" are often used interchangeably (and are used interchangeably in this dissertation study, as well) to describe "forms of racism that are pervasively and deeply embedded in and throughout systems, laws, written or unwritten policies, entrenched practices, and established beliefs and attitudes that produce, condone, and perpetuate widespread unfair treatment of people of color" (Braveman et al., 2022, p. 172). The term, "racism" is primarily used in this study to denote all forms of racism.

Racism may be perpetuated in nursing education through the curriculum (Dillard-Wright et al., 2023; Idehuru-Anderson & Alexander, 2022). Curriculum is the mechanism through which assumptions and expectations are conveyed to students, either formally, informally, or through omission (Boston College, 2021). Duman's (2023) research report on metaphors describing null

curriculum discussed the etiology and the various understandings of "curriculum" (Duman,

2023, p. 2274). The formal curriculum is a document that includes items such as course contents,

teaching strategies, and anticipated learning outcomes designed for implementing an

instructional course. How the instructor implements or teaches the formal curriculum is the

explicit curriculum. The implicit curriculum includes those things that are taught, such as

traditions and values, that are not included in the formal curriculum (Duman, 2023). The implicit

curriculum, also known as the hidden curriculum, was described by the Teaching and Writing

center of Boston College as:

> an amorphous collection of implicit academic, social, and cultural messages, unwritten
>
> rules and unspoken expectations, and unofficial norms, behaviors and values of the
>
> dominant-culture context in which all teaching and learning is situated. These
>
> assumptions and expectations that are not formally communicated, established, or
>
> conveyed stipulate the 'right' way to think, speak, look, and behave in school (Boston
>
> College, 2021, para. 1).

Duman's (2023) study focused on the null curriculum, characterizing it as "what is missing, left

out, or overlooked…forms of knowledge that have been omitted" (Duman, 2023, p. 2275).

Subjects in the null curricula may be intentionally omitted by decision-makers (a school district's

forbidding the teaching of history with references to slavery might be an example); omitted by

implementation (the information is available, but the teacher chooses not to teach it); or ignored

by the student experientially (things in the curriculum that are not of interest to the student are

not done by the student). Participants in the Duman (2023) study produced multiple metaphors

for the null curriculum that were grouped into several themes with themes. Outstanding conclusions of the Duman (2023) study were that participants were aware of the null curriculum, participants felt the null curriculum was important, and that the curriculum was not complete because of the null curriculum. Consideration of the Duman (2023) study results laid groundwork for this dissertation study's discussion of what is included in nursing curriculum and an ensuing discussion in Chapter II about the exclusion of antiracism from nursing curriculum. Some nursing education scholars have insisted that nursing curriculum is Eurocentric (Bell, 2021; Hamzavi & Brown, 2023) or centered on Whiteness (Dillard-Wright et al., 2023; Idehuru-Anderson & Alexander, 2022; Puzan, 2003). Studies around representation of race and skin tone in nursing and medical textbooks found that the diversity of skin tones among racial and ethnic groups in the U.S. was not reflective of the population, with lighter skin tones being overrepresented in the texts (Louie & Wilkes, 2018; Pusey-Reid et al., 2023). *Whiteness* signifies a general understanding in the U.S. that the only valid experience is the experience of White people (Sawyer & Waite, 2021). Implications of a curriculum centered on Whiteness for Black nursing students are explored in Ch. II. Review of the Literature.

There is a fair amount known from the literature about Black students' experiences with racism in nursing school at PWIs. Among the articles that describe Black students' experiences with racism in predominately White nursing programs are the Ackerman-Barger et al. (2020) study on racial microaggressions, the White et al. (2020) qualitative study describing of 14 African American students' experiences with mistrust in nursing school, and the White and Fulton (2015) integrative literature review that identified common experiences among African American nursing students. One of the few studies found that discussed White faculty's understanding of racism was the Akamine Phillips et al. (2019) study addressing personal and professional barriers faced by White faculty who identified as "antiracist allies" (Akamine

Phillips et al., 2019, p. 6). There is a scarcity of data on nursing educators' understanding of effects of racism on Black students at Predominately White Institutions (PWIs). Yet, what nursing educators at PWIs know and experience themselves with racism may influence how they approach their educational practice and may have an impact on the educational experiences of Black nursing students. This qualitative phenomenological research study focuses on exploring nursing educators' meanings of the lived experience of racism and their perceptions of the effects of racism on Black nursing students. This research is necessary, as it adds to the paucity of existing documentation on the intersection of nursing educators at PWIs, racism, and Black nursing students (Bell, 2021; Iheduru-Anderson & Alexander, 2022). Chapter II includes a more detailed discussion of the topic.

Problem Statement

There is a lack of data on nursing educators' understanding of racism and the impacts of racism on Black students. Attrition of Black nursing students at Predominately White Institutions (PWIs) is a problem, particularly considering the on-going shortage of nurses in the United States. Racism experienced in nursing school may create barriers between Black students and graduation from nursing programs at PWIs. It is assumed that nursing educators at PWIs seek to create safe and inclusive teaching and learning spaces for all their students (Miller & Vaughn, 2023; Pusey-Reid et al., 2022). However, there is a dearth of evidentiary documentation that nursing educators at PWIs create inclusive spaces, or recognize the need to create such spaces, to alleviate the impact of racism on Black nursing students. Also missing from current literature is evidence of nursing educators at PWIs' meanings of the phenomenon of racism.

Purpose of the Study

The purpose of this study is to address a gap in the literature related to nursing educators and Black students at Predominately White Institutions (PWIs) by exploring nursing educators' meanings of the phenomenon of racism and their understanding of the effects of racism on Black nursing students (Bell, 2021; White et al., 2020). The study's purpose relates to the problem of attrition of Black nursing students at PWIs in the midst of an on-going nursing shortage. This research explored the experiences of nursing faculty, staff, and administrators at Predominately White Institutions (PWIs) through an online qualitative survey and individual interviews. The researcher approached this study through the lens of Critical Race Theory (CRT) with a spirit of inquiry to gather information and gain understanding of the phenomenon of racism from nursing educators. Anticipated outcomes of this study were that nursing educators would "examine the ways racist thoughts and feelings have permeated our consciousness, teaching, and curriculum" (Iheduru-Anderson & Alexander, 2022, p. 8) and that they would be encouraged to seek solutions to support Black nursing students, alleviate the nursing shortage and add to the diversity of the workforce.

Research Questions

The following research questions were developed to better understand the phenomenon of racism as understood and experienced by nursing faculty, staff, and administrators (collectively referred to from here forward as "nursing educators" in this study) at Predominately White Institutions (PWIs):

RQ1: What are nursing educators at Predominately White Institutions' (PWIs) meanings of the lived experience of racism?

RQ2: How do nursing educators at Predominately White Institutions (PWIs) perceive the effects or impact of racism on Black nursing students?

The questions, separately and taken together, addressed gaps in nursing education literature. This research situates RQ1 and RQ2 within the theoretical framework of Critical Race Theory (CRT), with the following essential assumptions:

- Racism is "ordinary; not aberrational" (Delgado & Stefancic, 2017, p. 8).

- Narratives are the "cure for silencing" (Delgado & Stefancic, 2017, p. 50).

- Discussing their experiences with race and racism may help nursing educators' better understand and address the needs of Black nursing students.

Implicit in the CRT tenet of the normalcy of racism in the U.S. is the concept of colorblindness that allows White individuals to be unaware of the existence and effects of racism (Dancis & Coleman, 2022). This research was approached with a spirit of inquiry and with an understanding that there may be nursing educators at PWIs, particularly White nursing educators, who may lack knowledge about racism, based on their personal patterns of knowing (Chinn et al., 2022) and their own socialization into nursing education (Dancis & Coleman, 2022). Approaching research with a spirit of inquiry, "an ongoing curiosity about the best evidence to guide [clinical] decision making" (Melnyk et al., 2009), is a respected practice in nursing education science.

Theoretical Framework

The researcher approached this dissertation research study through the lens of Critical Race Theory (CRT). CRT is a way of thinking propounded by several sources, several of whom will be mentioned and examined in Chapter II. Review of the Literature. Prominently featured among the sources to be discussed in the next chapter are the works of Derrick Bell, Kimberlé Crenshaw, Neil Gotanda, Richard Delgado and Jean Stefancic. This dissertation research was considered in the context of the first tenet of CRT which stresses the omnipresence and routineness of racism in American culture (Delgado & Stefancic, 2017) and the reasoning that many White people have been able, through colorblindness, to ignore the phenomenon of racism and its effects on Black people in America (Brown University, 2015; Delgado & Stefancic, 2017; Mills, 2022b). Critical Race Theory is presented in detail in Chapter II. Review of the Literature with a discussion of the significance of the framework to this study on understanding nursing educators' meanings of the lived experience of racism. The researcher selected CRT as a theoretical framework, with an understanding that CRT is more of a broad lens for looking at society than it is a theory.

Assumptions and Limitations

Assumptions

The researcher's assumptions for this study follow:

- Racism exists and is prevalent in nursing education, as it is everywhere else in U.S. society (Iheduru-Anderson & Wahi, 2022; Waddell-Henowitch et al., 2022).

- By definition, the student population of PWIs is mostly White; therefore, Black students comprise the minority population at PWIs (American Association of Colleges of Nursing [AACN], 2023a, section P).

- Black nursing students have additional stressors beyond the commonly known stressors of nursing students. These stressors are related to racism, bias, and discrimination that impact Black nursing students (Attis-Josias, 2023; Matthews et al., 2022).

- "Because of the historical vestiges of slavery, segregation, and legalized discrimination, Black people face more, and qualitatively different, discrimination and devaluation than do other POC in the United States" (Hall & Fields, 2012, p. 27); Black Americans have been historically and "remain politically, economically, and racially disadvantaged relative to their White counterparts" (McClain, 2021, p. 493).

- Nursing faculty and administrators at PWIs are mostly White people (Tobbell, 2023).

- It was the author's personal observation that staff have regular communication with students, in some cases more than faculty and administrators; administrators may or may not have much contact with students, depending on their roles. Administrators usually have experience as faculty prior to becoming administrators. They are included in this conversation as their perspective adds to the thickness of the data and the upper-level decision making.

- Proponents of Critical Race Theory emphasize the importance of sharing counternarratives, hearing the stories of Brown and Black people about their experiences with White people and with racism (Delgado & Stefancic, 2017). Black nursing students' narratives are abundant in current literature (Ackerman-Barger & Hummel, 2015; Ackerman-Barger et al., 2020; Attis-Josias, 2023; Bell, 2021; Childs et al., 2004; Matthews et al., 2022; White & Fulton, 2015; White et al., 2020). This study's aim was to approach narratives from a fresh perspective and hear those of nursing educators, as they those individuals are, essentially, the gatekeepers of the profession (Hamzavi & Brown, 2023). This strategy may not only bring a fresh perspective to nursing education literature but may also raise awareness for the reader of the issues presented here.

- Nursing education is multi-faceted and complex and difficult to describe and summarize in one work (Chinn et al., 2022). Collecting narratives by hearing from individuals currently employed in the profession of nursing education is extremely valuable to the work of knocking down racial barriers, creating equitable and inclusive learning environments, and, possibly, to getting more Black students to graduation (Ackerman-Barger & Hummel, 2015).

Limitations

Limitations of this study included the possibility that respondents would be uncomfortable verbalizing their reflections on race and racism. Racism is a "sensitive and potentially traumatic topic" (Borowsky, 2023, p. 287). The researcher anticipated that her race and her familiarity with nursing education and with some of the participants and their worksites might have helped or hindered the inquiry process. The researcher was at risk for experiencing "vicarious trauma" (Borowsky, 2023, p. 288) while conducting this study. As a phenomenological study, the results of this study were not expected to be generalizable. Generalizability and other measures of validity are discussed in detail in Chapter III.

A Word About Use of Racial and Ethnic Terms in This Dissertation

The terms, "Black", "White", and other designations for racial and ethnic groups are capitalized throughout this dissertation, as they are considered proper nouns by the American Psychological Association (APA), (2020). Terms used in paraphrased selections and direct quotations that were not capitalized in the original work may be capitalized here for convenience and out of respect for people in those groups, unless this researcher sensed that capitalizing will alter the original intent of the message. "White" is often written with a lower case "w" (District of Columbia [DC] Office of Racial Equity, 2022, p. 3). The author made every effort to capitalize every instance of the word "White" unless, as stated above, the lower case was used in a quotation and capitalizing will alter the intent of the original author. The researcher preferred not to use the designation "minority" as a noun to represent Black people but retained that terminology if it was part of a quoted or paraphrased selection from the literature. The same was true of terms such as "BIPOC" and "non-White". BIPOC is an acronym for "Black, Indigenous and other persons of color" and refers to people in the United States that have been "racialized" historically; "BIPOC" and "non-White" are terms used to describe people who are not White (DC Office of Racial Equity, 2022, p. 5; Meraji, Escobar, & Devarajan, 2020).

The researcher used the terms "Black" and "African American" people together at times throughout the report to illustrate that those terms are sometimes used interchangeably in the literature, and among members of those ethnic groups. The term "Black" was the preferred term for this author as its use represents for this researcher, as well as for many other Black people, a "sense of pride and empowerment" (DC Office of Racial Equity, 2022, p. 5). "Black" also embodies "the unique Black experience in America, regardless of national origin" (DC Office of Racial Equity, 2022, p. 5). "Black" persons as viewed in this dissertation study refer to persons born, raised, and educated in the U.S., descendants of enslaved people, and still experiencing the fallout of the system of slavery (Horowitz, 2019). Black nursing students in this dissertation study were Black individuals enrolled in nursing programs in the United States.

Significance of the Study

Through phenomenological inquiry, this study sought to explore meanings of the lived experience of racism with nursing educators at Predominately White Institutions (PWIs) and to discover nursing educators' perceptions of the effects of racism on Black nursing students. Perhaps this study will contribute to a better understanding of which experiences in nursing school influence attrition and success of Black nursing students (Gates, 2018; White et al., 2020). There is a "paucity of nursing education research" (Halstead & Frank, 2017, p. 4). This research study focused on nursing education, specifically on nursing faculty, staff, and administrators to provide various perspectives and a holistic view. Not well-documented in the literature are the meanings of racism for nursing educators and their knowledge of (or acknowledgement of) the impact of racism on Black students. Documenting this exploration of the meaning of the lived experience of racism for nursing educators at PWIs, may add to existing knowledge about nursing educators' roles in preparing future nurses. This dissertation study is significant as it may engage the reader in seeking solutions that may alleviate the nursing shortage and add to the diversity of the workforce.

This study's findings and themes from the literature discussed in this study, particularly those related to RQ 1 and RQ 2 that spoke to nursing educators' perceptions and meaning-making, may be of interest to nursing education scientists, nursing faculty, staff, and administrators of nursing education programs. Understanding the perspectives of nursing faculty, staff and administrators may be beneficial in developing strategies for recruiting and retaining nursing students of color.

Subjectivity Statement

This researcher is a Black woman who currently teaches undergraduate nursing at a Predominately White Institution (PWI) in the Mid-Atlantic region of the United States. Her values align with the values of community, respect, and inclusivity expressed in the mission statements of the institutions where she works and where she is earning her doctorate. She acknowledges that there are many levels of racism— systemic, structural, institutional, personal —and that issues around race and ethnicity are woven throughout the fabric of U.S. society. Racism has profound effects on the psyche, behaviors, perceptions, perceptions of, and treatment of Black people in the United States. Taking a "colorblind" approach to anti-Black racism and treating all people as being the same does not address the healthcare and educational disparities created by structural racism (Adeniran et al., 2023). To take such an approach is to willfully ignore one's own biases and to disregard the positionality and the needs of groups of people who have historically been marginalized in the United States because of the color of their skin (Iheduru-Anderson & Alexander, 2022). Prioritizing cultural competence and multiculturism over actively implementing anti-racism merely places Whiteness in the center of nursing education and has not challenged racism (Bell, 2021; Blanchet Garneau et al., 2018; Iheduru-Anderson & Wahi, 2022; Iheduru-Anderson & Waite, 2022), nor has it corrected the problem of attrition of Black students. To address this gap, this dissertation project revolves around two key research questions (RQ 1 and RQ 2) which situates this study in relation to the lens of Critical Race Theory (CRT) and an understanding that some nursing faculty, staff, and administrators at PWIs may truly lack knowledge about racism, based on their socialization into nursing education (Dancis & Coleman, 2022). The researcher remains optimistic that nursing faculty are amenable to learning new ways of doing things, particularly when they are supported in their continuing education with structure and policy and time and space to learn (Adeniran et al., 2023; Chen et al., 2020; Dzurec, 2022; Ohito, 2016). The researcher concurs with Ladson-Billings (University of North Carolina Asheville [UNCA], 2015), on interest convergence— that people will make the adjustments they need when they understand how those adjustments benefit them.

The inquiry for this dissertation study was approached from the perspective that individuals participating in this study have already shown their commitment to caring for other people by choosing a caring profession (Waddell-Henowitch et al., 2022). In studying the phenomenon of racism and nursing educators' understanding of its effects on Black students at PWIs, the researcher expressed the same belief as Dancis and Coleman (2022) that knowledge and understanding disrupt and dispel racism. So then, with knowledge, colorblindness and ignorance can no longer be accepted as the norm in nursing education (Waddell-Henowitch et al.,

2022). The researcher addressed the epistemology of such ignorance (Dancis & Coleman, 2022) through the research design afforded through RQ1's emphasis on the lived experience of racism and RQ2's exploration of the perception of the effects of racism as well as any other personal positionality that arises during the study through reflexive practices. The researcher recognized the need to maintain compassion (Rundell, 2023) and a spirit of inquiry (Melnyk et al., 2009) during this process of discovery with trusted colleagues and mentors and intended to keep a personal journal throughout the study.

Definition of Terms

Antiracist— "One who is expressing an idea of racial equality or is actively supporting a policy that leads to racial equity or justice" (Kendi, 2016, p. 15)

Anti-racist education/pedagogy— "a commitment to educate students in ways that make racialized power relations explicit, deconstruct the social construction of race, and analyze interlocking systems of oppression that serve to marginalize and exclude some groups while privileging others" (Hassouneh, 2006, as cited in Iheduru-Anderson & Waite, 2022, p. 11)

Attrition—is described as exiting, dropping out, leaving a nursing program or "non-completion" of the course of study in nursing school (Wray et al., 2017, p. 16).

Best practices—"health practices, methods, interventions, procedures, or techniques based on high-quality evidence in order to obtain improved patient and health outcomes…evidence alone is not sufficient to ensure evidence-based decision making but requires uptake and sustained implementation of the evidence" (ten Ham-Baloyi et al., 2020)

Black or African American—"typically refers to the ethnicity, nationality, and culture of Black people residing in or born in the United States" (Mitchell, 2023, p. 86) and is specific to their experience.

Colorblindness—"the denial of racial inequalities by those who do not 'see' color and fail to take racism into account" (Hall & Fields, 2012, p. 26)

Cultural competency—refers to studying a specific culture with the goal of obtaining a set of instructions on how to work with people of that culture (Wesp et al., 2018). The term "cultural competence" may be found in the same conversations as terms such as "multicultural", "diversity" and cultural "differences" (Bell, 2021, p. 3; Davis & O'Brien, 2020, p. 562); Cultural competency is criticized as it emphasizes "power dynamics and perceiving non-Whites as 'other'…validates assumed inferiority of the marginalized group" (Iheduru-Anderson & Waite, 2022, p. 2).

Diversity— "encompasses differences in race, age, gender, religion, culture, language, sex, and socioeconomic class of individual persons" (Green, 2020, p. 280). "'Diversity' is used in place of any critical discussion of racialization and racism" (Bell, 2021, p. 6).

Equity— "examines the fairness by which persons of diverse backgrounds are able to access information, higher education, and resources that help them to advance and fully contribute to society" (Green, 2020, p. 280).

Evidence-based teaching practice—"validation, generation, application, and perpetuation of those methods that facilitate the preparation of skilled and thoughtful nurses who function in a constantly evolving, global health care environment. It is the incorporation of the *doing* of the teaching with the *study* of the teaching" (Emerson & Records, 2008, p. 361).

Hidden curriculum—"an amorphous collection of implicit academic, social, and cultural messages, unwritten rules and unspoken expectations, and unofficial norms, behaviors and values of the dominant-culture context in which all teaching and learning is situated. These assumptions and expectations that are not formally communicated, established, or conveyed stipulate the 'right' way to think, speak, look, and behave in school" (Boston College, 2021, para. 1).

Historically Black Colleges and Universities (HBCUs)—institutions of higher education in the U.S. founded with the intent of educating Black people amidst Black people's exclusion from other (Predominantly White Institutions [PWIs]. HBCUs continue to provide safe spaces for Black students to obtain a quality education and be exposed to Black culture (Clayton et al., 2023).

Inclusion—"an environment that offers affirmation, celebration, and appreciation of different approaches, styles, perspectives, and experiences, thus allowing all individuals to bring in their whole selves (and all their identities) and to demonstrate their strengths and capacity" (American Psychological Association [APA], 2023, p. 6).

Interest convergence—"a way to make the interests of people of color intersect with those of Whites" (UNCA, 2015). Interest convergence is a premise of CRT and contends that legislation and policy that are anti-racist only happen if they benefit White people. "Interest convergence asserts that decisions regarding equity and civil rights are more likely to occur when the subordinate group can align its interests with those of the dominant group" (UNCA, 2015).

Intersectionality—is related to the CRT tenet of differential racialization. Kimberlé Crenshaw is credited with introducing the term in essays on Black women's employment and violence against Black women, which involves the various ways race, gender, and class intersected, (Crenshaw, 1995, p. 358).

Marginalized—"relegate[d] to an unimportant position of powerless position within a society or group" (Merriam-Webster, 2024).

Microaggressions—"Microaggressions are subtle slights, snubs, or insults that are either intentional or unintentional; they convey hostile, derogatory, or otherwise negative messages to target persons based on their membership in a structurally oppressed social group" (Carter & Phillips, 2021). "The means by which the personal (subjective) and social environmental dialectic of racism is carried on in everyday interactions, with little to no awareness on the part of White interactors, in specific social situations" (Hall & Fields, 2012, p. 26).

Nursing faculty—educate future nurses, advance the science of nursing education, and influence healthcare through teaching, scholarly work and service (Mariani, 2022).

People of color—Used instead of the term "minority" to refer to individuals from diverse racial and ethnic backgrounds. "Communities of color" is used when referring to groups from diverse backgrounds. The terms" underserved," "underrepresented," or "marginalized" also describe populations; but use of the specific group title is recommended, whenever possible. Examples include Black students, LGBTQ+ students, undocumented students (APA, 2021)

Positionality—individuals' position in society, in relation to their identity; informed by race, ethnicity, age, sexual orientation, ability, and other statuses; the intersection of our identities with systems of power, privilege and oppression (APA, 2021)

Predominately White Institutions (PWIs)—describes "institutions of higher learning in which White [students] account for 50% or greater of the student enrollment and whose histories, policies, and practices center the White majority" (AACN, 2023a, section P). PWIs have a history of barring Black students from attending (Clayton et al., 2023). Institutions that are not Historically Black Colleges or Universities (HBCUs), Primarily Black Institutions (PBIs), or other minority-serving institutions are considered PWIs (Clayton et al., 2023; Nguyen et al., 2023).

Race and Ethnicity—Race may be defined as a "social invention" used to classify people into groups based on "human differences associated with the different populations" (Wade et al., 2024, para. 7). Ethnicity "refers to a sense of identity and membership in a group that shares common language, cultural traits (values, beliefs, religion, food habits, customs, etc.), and a sense of a common history" (Wade et al., 2024, para. 12).

Racism—"the relegation of people of color to inferior status and treatment based on unfounded beliefs about innate inferiority, as well as unjust treatment and oppression of people of color, whether intended or not. Racism is not always conscious, intentional, or explicit—often it is systemic and structural" (Braveman et al., 2022, p. 171). Racism is "a system of structuring opportunity and assigning value based on phenotypic properties (e.g., skin color and hair texture associated with 'race' in the United States). This 'system'—which ranges from daily interpersonal interactions shaped by race to racialized opportunities for good education, housing, employment, and so forth—unfairly disadvantages people belonging to marginalized racial groups and damages their physical and mental health, and unfairly advantages individuals belonging to socially and politically dominant racial groups" (APA, 2021, p. 14). Kendi (2016) stated that his book, *Stamped*, is based on "anti-Black racist ideas", and racism refers to "any idea suggesting that Black people, or any group of Black people, are inferior in any way to another racial group (Kendi, 2016, p. 5).

STEM education—"the acronym STEM has been used to refer to the fields of science, technology, mathematics, and engineering…various iterations of the acronym (e.g., STEAM) have extended to encompass agriculture, the arts, the environment, economics, education, and medicine… The acronym also has been adopted by governments, educators, businesses, communities, and industry leaders to communicate an urgent need for educating students and preparing them for college and the workforce…commonly described as an interdisciplinary approach to learning where rigorous academic concepts are coupled with real-world lessons" (Srikoom et al., 2018, p. 313).

Systemic racism—"emphasizes the involvement of whole systems, and often all systems—for example, political, legal, economic, health care, school, and criminal justice systems—including the structures that uphold the systems" (Braveman et al., 2022, p. 172).

Structural racism – "structural racism emphasizes the role of the structures (laws, policies, institution-al practices, and entrenched norms) that are the systems' scaffolding" (Braveman et al., 2022, p. 172).

White ignorance—A term was coined by philosopher, Charles W. Mills in his seminal 1997 work, *The Racial Contract* (Mills, 2022b), and later elaborated upon in a volume of essays on epistemologies of ignorance and race (Mills, 2007). A state in which some White people and other people who see Whiteness as normative do not know, choose not to acknowledge, or suppress of the truth about the racialized world created by White people.

White privilege—"an invisible package of unearned assets that I can count on cashing in each day, but about which I was 'meant' to remain oblivious. White privilege is like an invisible weightless knapsack of special provisions, maps, passports, codebooks, visas, clothes, tools, and blank checks" (McIntosh & Cleveland, 1990, para. 3). "Since White people in America hold most of the political, institutional, and economic power, they receive advantages that non-White groups do not. These benefits and advantages, of varying degrees, are known as White privilege" (National Museum of African American History and Culture [NMAAHC], n.d., para. 7).

White supremacy—"the racist belief that White people are superior to people of other races and that they should have power over them" (Allcorn, 2021, p. 280). "White supremacy and racism are deeply woven into the fabric of American society" (Allcorn, 2021, p. 284).

Whiteness—"quality pertaining to Euro-American or Caucasian people or traditions" (Delgado & Stefancic, 2017, p. 186). Whiteness is a powerful social category "within a racialized social system" (Mills, 2022a, para. 1). "Whiteness and White racialized identity refer to the way that White people, their customs, culture, and beliefs operate as the standard by which all other groups of are compared…a culture where nonwhite persons are seen as inferior or abnormal" (NMAAHC, n.d., para. 3). "… it is generally gleaned that the White experience and the White narrative are essentially the only ones" (Sawyer & Waite, 2021, p. 4). In a key essay on Critical Race Theory, Cheryl I. Harris discussed Whiteness as property and described it as a valuable possession, symbolizing freedom, that yielded benefits for the holder (Harris, 1995).

Chapter I introduced the proposed study with the problem of the lack of data on nursing educators' understanding of racism and the barriers racism creates between Black students at PWIs and graduation from nursing school. It provided a brief overview of the challenges faced by Black students in nursing education. It further introduced the problem of attrition related to marginalization and feelings of isolation and related attrition to the problem of the on-going nursing shortage. This introduction focused on students and nursing educators in prelicensure programs at Predominately White Institutions (PWIs). Nursing educators were defined in this chapter as faculty, staff, and administrators that work with students in nursing programs. Their roles were briefly described here in Chapter 1. The purpose of the study was given – to gain insight of nursing educators' understanding of racism and its impact on Black nursing students – followed by research questions related to the problem statement and the purpose of the study. A brief description of the theoretical framework, Critical Race Theory, followed. This framework supports ideas about nursing educators' lack of understanding about the phenomenon of racism and about racism being a barrier for Black nursing students and justifies the research being conducted. The significance of the study was stated as contributing to the literature on nursing educators' knowledge of racism and the effects on their students. This study may be significant to the call for nursing educators to incorporate antiracist practices in their teaching and praxes as it approaches the topic from the educators' perspective. The results of this study will add to the body of knowledge about nursing educators and may be one of the few to include the narratives of nursing program staff. The researcher's positionality was revealed in the Subjectivity Statement. Finally, an extensive Definition of Terms was provided. Chapter II offers an exhaustive review of literature related to the problem to be addressed by this study and provides an in-depth presentation of the theoretical framework. Chapter III focuses on the study's methodology and ethical considerations and further explains the positionality and role of the researcher. Chapter IV is a detailed discussion of the findings of the study, and Chapter V concludes the study with discussions of findings, implications, and recommendations.

Chapter II. Literature Review

This chapter's literature review begins with a discussion of the problems of the nursing shortage, attrition of Black nursing students, racial microaggressions in nursing education, and systemic racism external to nursing education that may affect Black nursing students' ability to succeed at predominately White nursing programs. The first section underscores the significance of the nursing shortage and articulates a vision for a future of nursing that considers a growing and increasingly diverse United States population. The next section reviews literature related to Black students' not completing predominately White nursing programs and relates attrition to the nursing shortage and to the practices mentioned in the following section. This discussion continues with racial microaggressions and other ways that nursing educators at PWIs may exclude Black nursing students, unawares. A brief discussion of racism in the U.S. is justified, with the researcher considering Black nursing students holistically and reviewing related literature from the position that nursing students may be affected by what is happening in the world outside of campus and might not easily separate those influences from their experiences in the nursing educational setting. Background information on nursing and nursing educators is provided for the benefit of readers who are unfamiliar with the profession and with the complexities of preparing students to become practicing nurses. An explication of nursing education practices follows, with subtopics on knowledge dissemination and transfer. Topics related to the nursing curriculum are discussed in the next section to establish an overview of normative practices in nursing education, practices which tend to overlook systemic inquiry into racism. This backdrop provides an essential foundation upon which to rest its two primary research questions: first probing the understanding and meaning of the lived experience of racism of nursing faculty, staff, and administrators at PWIs (RQ1) then examining nursing educators' perceptions as they reflect on the effects or impact of racism on Black nursing students at PWIs. The chapter then offers readers a review of the literature on Whiteness in the nursing curriculum, socialization into the profession, and the inclusion of cultural competency in nursing curriculum and connects nursing educators and their practices to Black students' experiences with racism in nursing. A discussion of Critical Race Theory as a theoretical framework for this study rounds out Chapter II, for it is suggested that this approach may have implications for addressing the problem of attrition of Black nursing students at PWIs within the ongoing shortage of nurses more generally.

Problems

Nursing Shortage

The COVID-19 pandemic exacerbated an existing shortage of nurses and nursing faculty in the United States (Caravelis et al., 2023; Lopez et al., 2022; Mariani, 2022; Yordy, 2006). During the pandemic, which was declared by the World Health Organization (WHO) on March 11, 2020, the number of nurses leaving or intending to leave the profession was alarmingly high (See et al., 2023). New nurses planned to leave the profession during the pandemic at a higher rate than experienced nurses. The mass exodus from nursing left a gap of 4.7 million positions globally that needed to be filled by new nursing graduates (Lopez et al., 2022). Prior to the pandemic, it was known that one-third of the estimated 3 million nurses working in the U.S. were expected to retire or leave their jobs between 2017 and 2030 (Walters et al., 2022). To prepare the numbers of new nurses needed to fill positions that are expected to be vacated, the United States needs nursing students to graduate nursing school, pass their state licensure exams, and become registered nurses.

As the U.S. population becomes increasingly diverse, it is more important now than ever that the nursing workforce reflects the cultural diversity of the nation (Green, 2020). While more than 13% of the U.S. population identifies as Black or African American, only about 6% of registered nurses are Black (AACN, 2023b; White et al., 2020). The call for more inclusion of underrepresented groups in nursing education is grounded in evidence that a more diverse nursing workforce will contribute to a decrease in healthcare inequities among various groups of people (Campaign for Action, 2023; Matthews et al., 2022; National Academies of Sciences et al., 2021; Phillips & Malone, 2014). Alsan et al. (2019) highlighted the importance of diversifying the healthcare workforce. Their experimental study on the demand for preventive care among African American men showed that Black men were more likely to accept invasive preventive care such as diabetes screenings and flu vaccines from Black male doctors. The researchers predicted that increased screening encouraged by the presence of Black physicians could reduce mortality among Black men (Alsan et al., 2019). Accordingly, African American nurses have always been integral to the health of their communities. They provided care for Black communities long before they were accepted into White schools of nursing and were allowed access to licensure and employment in White hospitals (White & Fulton, 2015).

Attrition

Attrition, or non-completion of nursing school, is high among students from underrepresented groups in nursing education (Harris et al., 2014; Kubec, 2017; Matthews et al., 2022). Attrition is a problem for the U.S. nursing workforce (Eudy & Brooks, 2022). It is estimated that almost half of nursing students of color in some areas of the U.S. leave their programs without graduating (Henderson et al., 2020; Kubec, 2017). This is consistent with the U.S. rate of attrition for students of color in higher education (U.S. Department of Education,

2023). Harris et al. (2014) identified risk factors for nursing students enrolled in an associate degree program located within a Historically Black College and University (HBCU) in the Midwest. They reported that attrition rates were "exceedingly high and problematic for many programs" (Harris et al., p. 32). Other, major barriers for minority nursing students uncovered in the Harris et al. (2014) study were struggling academically in the Anatomy and Physiology, a requisite course for nursing, failing a nursing course early in the nursing program, scoring less than 76% on any exam, working more than 16 to 20 hours a week, lack of faculty support, and nursing programs' failure to understand the cultural needs of minority nursing students. Although persisting to graduation is challenging for all nursing students, Black students have an especially difficult time (Harris et al., 2014; White & Fulton, 2015; White et al., 2020). Causal factors associated with attrition of Black students at PWIs are both academic and social. Some of the reasons Black students drop out of nursing school are experiences with discrimination, bias, and microaggressions; feelings of isolation; issues with communication; lack of academic, technical, and social support; and lack of role models (Eudy & Brooks, 2022; Matthews et al., 2022). This research project used qualitative approaches including online qualitative surveys and structured interviews to explore some of these issues and themes through articulation of lived experiences.

Racial Microaggressions and Other Related Behaviors in Nursing

Carter and Phillips (2021) wrote an article endorsing a revolutionary revision of the nursing curriculum to identify and dismantle structures that support racism in nursing education. They reminded nursing educators that they own the nursing curriculum and had the power to make it into a curriculum that would lead to fair and equitable treatment for Black and Brown nursing students and for patients. Carter and Phillips (2021) recommended that knowledge about recognizing and responding to microaggressions be included in the nursing curriculum. They defined microaggressions as "subtle slights, snubs, or insults that are either intentional or unintentional; they convey hostile, derogatory, or otherwise negative messages to target persons based on their membership in a structurally oppressed social group" (Carter & Phillips, 2021, p. 26). Ladson-Billings referred to microaggressions as a "thousand daily cuts" in a 2015 talk at University of North Carolina Asheville (UNCA, 2015).

Ackerman-Barger et al. (2020) identified racial microaggressions as forms of exclusion and marginalization that are distinguished from blatant, racist attacks by their subtlety. Although the term "micro" was used to refer to these behaviors, the effects of microaggressions are anything but small and meaningless. Racial microaggressions, even if they were not intentional on the part of the perpetrator, threatened the well-being and academic performance of the nursing and medical students in the Ackerman-Barger et al. (2020) study. Ackerman and Barger conducted focus groups with 37 "underrepresented HP [health professions] students from two prestigious Predominately White Institutions (PWIs). They found that "chronic racial microaggressions create stress which, cumulatively, can wear down cognitive function, flatten self-esteem, impair productivity, and damage relationships – all of which can lead to diminished learning and academic performance" (Ackerman-Barger et al., 2020, p. 759). This dissertation project similarly draws upon phenomenological research to explore participants' experiences at PWIs.

Faculty, staff, and administrators of nursing programs may be unconscious of the things they say or do that may cause harmful effects on their students (Ackerman-Barger et al., 2020). Nursing educators may not recognize or understand the barriers their Black students face related to racism (Eudy & Brooks, 2022; Green, 2020; Tobbell, 2023). It was the aim of this research project to help address this gap in understanding, particularly across a range of perspectives –

faculty, staff, and administrators.

What Black Students Say about their Nursing School Experiences

Several studies have documented the experiences of Black students at PWIs (Ackerman-

Barger & Hummel, 2015; Ackerman-Barger et al., 2020; Attis-Josias, 2023; Bell, 2021; Childs et

al., 2004; White & Fulton, 2015; White et al., 2020). Black students in those studies described

the institutional climate of nursing schools as lonely (Childs et al., 2004; White & Fulton, 2015),

inhospitable (Ackerman-Barger & Hummel, 2015), riddled with stereotyping and mistrust

(White et al., 2020), and unsupportive (Bell, 2021). Students of color at PWIs have reported

being isolated and marginalized by faculty in nursing school and feeling stress from being treated

differently from other students (Ackerman-Barger et al., 2020; Attis-Josias, 2023; White &

Fulton, 2015; White et al., 2020). One such treatment was being singled out in class as an expert

on a particular culture and called upon to teach White students about that culture, also known as

the diversity tax (Ackerman-Barger & Hummel, 2015; Ackerman-Barger et al., 2020). Having

their opinions and contributions minimized and devalued were other treatments which affected

learning and well-being of students of color in nursing school (Ackerman-Barger et al., 2020).

Nursing students of color have shared their struggles with not being able to relate to White

faculty and have bemoaned the lack of faculty of color with whom they could connect (Attis-

Josias, 2023). They reported being humiliated by White instructors and having their

contributions to group projects minimized and work plagiarized by classmates (Ackerman-

Barger & Hummel, 2015). In a qualitative descriptive study, White et al. (2020) described the

racial experiences of 14 African American students at predominately European American

prelicensure nursing schools. Major themes yielded from secondary analysis of data were trust and mistrust. African American students characterized mistrust as their being guarded in their interactions with European American faculty. Their sense of mistrust was attributed to faculty engaging in stereotyping, faculty's actions being incongruent with their words, and faculty holding African American students to a different academic standard than European students (White et al., 2020). Students' reflections on trustful relationships with European American faculty included mentoring, faculty being present with students by listening intently and taking time with students and being "active in programs that promoted diversity within the school" (White et al., 2020, p. 160). Students in the Ackerman-Barger et al. (2020) study made the following suggestions for promoting inclusion in health profession schools: Diversify the faculty, staff, leadership, and student body and encourage allyship from among White people in the institution to promote diversity and inclusion; Reform the curriculum, deemphasizing race and ethnicity and increasing focus on social determinants of health and health equity; Include open discussions about race, ethnicity, and racism in the classroom; and create safe spaces for people to gather with other people of similar backgrounds (Ackerman-Barger et al., 2020). This dissertation research was similarly attuned to gathering stories of lived experiences, perceptions about the effect of racism, and the meanings ascribed to these experiences at PWIs.

Racism in the U.S.

A broader discussion of issues related to race in the U.S. is fitting here, for it may assist the reader in understanding the significance of this qualitative study's focus on nursing educators' meanings of the lived experience of racism and implications for Black nursing students. Racism in the U.S. is pervasive and involves entire systems such as the healthcare system and the educational system. Black nursing students are subject to the social contexts of the institutions they attend, and even those students residing on campus at the most inclusive colleges and universities, are not insulated from or immune to the racial injustices and violence that happen in the world outside of campus (Bell, 2021; Sumpter et al., 2023). Nursing students as well as nursing educators "do not operate in their professional role in isolation of their socialization, their socioeconomic and political contexts, nor their identities as racialized or non-racialized beings" (Bell, 2021, p. 2). This premise – and its wider socio-cultural and historical reality – informed the rationale for this dissertation's research design.

In April 2021, the Centers for Disease Control and Prevention (CDC) and the American Medical Association (AMA) declared racism a serious public health threat (Dancis & Coleman, 2022; Centers for Disease Control [CDC], 2023). This declaration came amid another public health crisis, the COVID-19 pandemic, which ravished Black communities and other communities of color in the U.S. at a disproportionately high rate. Racial and ethnic minority groups, particularly African American, Latino, and Native American, were disproportionately affected by COVID-19. Black Americans died at twice the rate of White Americans (Tai et al., 2021). The COVID-19 pandemic laid bare a myriad of healthcare disparities and social inequities caused by racism in the U.S. (Iheduru-Anderson & Alexander, 2022; Matthews et al., 2022). This crucible proved an added catalyst, and additional impetus for the social justice education dimension of this dissertation project.

The height of the COVID-19 pandemic was also a time of political turmoil and widespread civil unrest. After Americans watched a White police officer hold his knee on the neck of George Floyd, an unarmed Black man, for nine minutes and twenty-nine seconds, people took to the streets across the U.S and across the globe to protest that murder and other acts of senseless violence committed against people of color (History.com Editors, 2021; Iheduru-Anderson & Alexander, 2022; McClain, 2021). The climate in America was politically charged, with the President of the United States himself doing nothing to discourage racism, violence, and White supremacy (Allcorn, 2021). The country

> experienced more than four years of the presidency…that purposely exacerbated underlying racial tensions in the country. [The President's] words, policies, and actions made it acceptable to attack racial and ethnic minority groups, verbally as well as physically (McClain, 2021, p. 492).

On the heels of a divisive presidential administration and a deadly pandemic, on June 23, 2023, the Supreme Court of the United States decided to reverse affirmative action (*Students for Fair Admissions, Inc. v. President and Fellows of Harvard College*, 2023), eliminating race-based college admissions (Aaron et al., 2023). The outcome of that decision was that colleges and universities could no longer use race and ethnicity in their admissions decision-making (Liu, 2023). The Supreme Court decision was delivered at a time when enrolling and retaining Black students in higher education was already a concern. In anticipation of the June 23, 2023 decision of the Supreme Court of the United States to end race-conscious affirmative action policies (*Students for Fair Admissions, Inc. v. President and Fellows of Harvard College*, 2023), educational leaders wondered about "ramifications for medical training and health equity" (Aaron et al., 2023). The disenfranchisement of students of color was already evident in states where affirmative action policies were eliminated prior to 2023. Those states saw a decrease in college applications and enrollment of students of color (U.S. Department of Education, 2023). Universities that eliminated consideration of race and ethnicity as part of admissions decision-making saw a sharp decline not only in enrollment, but also in graduation rates of students of color (Murray & Noone, 2022). Similarly, "states with affirmative action bans saw a 4.8 percentage point decline in underrepresented racial and ethnic minority students in public medical schools" (Aaron et al., 2023, p. 2). The effect of that recent ruling on nursing programs remains to be seen. However, it is incumbent upon institutions to focus on retaining students of color and sustaining diverse learning environments (Hope & Munro, 2023). This dissertation study aimed to be part of this type of advocacy which is the underpinning for the two research questions that inform its design and methodology.

Iheduru-Anderson and Alexander (2022) challenged nurse educators to acknowledge structural racism in the U.S. and to confront their own biases so that they can better understand their students and prepare them to tackle health inequities and disparities in the workplace. They suggested incorporating CRT into the curriculum as a reimagination of nursing education. Applying the CRT framework to nursing education may help nursing educators and their students recognize the roles structural and institutionalized racism play in widening the disparities between White people and people of color. The application of CRT to the concepts of diversity, equity and inclusion in nursing education is salient for the current age and is overdue (Iheduru-Anderson & Alexander, 2022). Exploring nursing school faculty, staff, and administrators' perceptions of the effects of structural racism on Black nursing students at PWIs, as this dissertation project did, may be a small, but helpful, contribution to understanding how to better support the creation of inclusive learning spaces. Chronicling the narratives of the individuals working closely with Black students in mostly White spaces is an application of Critical Race Theory (CRT) and applies CRT to nursing education research (Iheduru-Anderson & Alexander, 2022).

Background Information on Nursing

This first section of the literature review chapter aimed to provide background and a context for those who are unfamiliar with nursing programs in the U.S. The information may also assist the reader to understand the environment in which nursing educators work. Nursing is complex and is not easily defined. There is no singular theoretical framework that wholly describes the discipline of nursing (AACN, 2021). National and international healthcare organizations provide synoptic definitions of nursing to assist the reader with a cursory understanding of the work of nurses. Nursing is the "…care of individuals of all ages, families, groups, and communities, sick or well and in all settings. Nursing includes the promotion of health, prevention of illness, and the care of ill, disabled and dying people" (International Council of Nurses [ICN], n.d. para. 1; World Health Organization [WHO], 2023, para. 1). The American Nurses Association (ANA) defined nursing in the context of time, as a journey with an individual patient through a healthcare continuum (American Nurses Association [ANA], n.d.-b). Nursing is further defined by the ANA (ANA, n.d.-b) as a specialized profession that is just as much an art as it is a science. The connection between viewing nursing as an art form, or an "aesthetic practice" (Chinn et al., 2022, p. 119) and nursing faculty's teaching practices are explored in Ch. II of this dissertation study. Common to the definitions of nursing is the idea that nurses carry out a plethora of tasks, and practice in a wide variety of professional settings (ANA, n.d.-a). The U.S. Bureau of Labor Statistics (2023) provided this overview of what registered nurses do:

> Assess patient health problems and needs, develop and implement nursing care plans, and maintain medical records. Administer nursing care to ill, injured, convalescent, or disabled patients. May advise patients on health maintenance and disease prevention or provide case management. Licensing or registration required (U.S. Bureau of Labor Statistics, 2023, para. 1).

In the U.S., nurses receive educational preparation for licensure and practice through nursing programs based at universities, colleges, community colleges, and hospitals. Upon graduation from an accredited nursing program, nursing students take an examination to qualify for licensure in the state where they wish to practice nursing (National Academies of Sciences et al., 2021). "Nursing education is the foundation of nursing practice" (Booth et al., 2016, p. 54). The educational setting where nurses prepare for their initial licensure is known as a pre-licensure program (nursing licenses must be renewed periodically and nurses may choose to pursue an advanced practice that requires an additional license). It is where nurses develop their professional identities, or perceptions of who they are individually as nurses, as well as their perceptions of what it means to be a nurse (Landis et al., 2022). The environment in which teaching and learning takes place and the educators' own identities and behaviors have implications for nursing students' educational experiences, their academic, social, and clinical outcomes and, eventually, the quality and longevity of their nursing careers (Harris, 2019; Walters et al., 2022). Such insights had applicability to this dissertation's line of inquiry and research method.

Nursing Educators

Staff

Information on staff of nursing programs is scant. Published reports on nursing program staff were not found. However, the importance of staff to the daily operation and the overall success of nursing education programs was implied in a couple of studies: Cary et al. (2020) omitted definitions of staff and delineation of staff roles, but described how staff was included with faculty and students in implementing the strategic plan to create a culture that valued diversity and inclusion at Duke University School of Nursing. The University of Illinois Chicago

College of Nursing named staff as stakeholders along with students and faculty and part of a

diversity strategic plan "to enhance the overall safety of the social climate and the educational

environment" of the institution (Matthews et al., 2022, p. 100). It was the dearth of information

on staff that this dissertation project planned to address through responses to RQ1.

Administrators

Administrators of nursing programs include "midlevel" (Sessler Branden & Sharts-

Hopko, 2017, p. 258) and "midcareer" (DeZure et al., 2014, p. 7) leadership positions such as

program director and department chair, and higher-level positions such as deans (DeZure et al.,

2014). Collectively, nursing administrators concern themselves with internal and external issues;

they stay abreast of current trends and forecasts in healthcare and develop vision and strategy,

and they seek the funding to move their organization forward for the future. Effective

communication is necessary with constituents at all levels of the organization as well as with

community partners. Nursing administrators are expected to have experience practicing nursing,

teaching, researching, and navigating new technology. Nursing administrators assure their

institution complies with state boards of nursing and accrediting bodies' regulations.

Administrators must be concerned externally with the nursing shortage, and internally with

admitting and retaining an adequate number of students to keep the budget balanced.

Administrators of nursing programs often advance to leadership roles by taking on tasks and

service activities that are in addition to their faculty roles (Berman, 2015; Bouws et al., 2020;

Green & Ridenour, 2004). This gap is one area that this dissertation study examined in some

detail as it includes this group's perception of their roles at PWIs.

Administrative roles require a different skillset from faculty roles. Most administrators in

nursing education have not had the academic preparation for academic leadership positions

(Berman, 2015). Evidence also shows that nursing faculty are often ambivalent about taking administrative leadership roles and are recruited or accept new roles out of a sense of obligation (Bouws et al., 2016; DeZure et al., 2014). In addition to the unanticipated amount of time and responsibility that accompanied a new administrative role, administrators reported that their relationships with fellow faculty changed with their advancement to leadership (Bouws et al., 2016; DeZure et al., 2014; Sessler Branden & Sharts-Hopko, 2017). Deans in the Bouws et al. (2016) study, while in top nursing education leadership roles at their institutions, reported hostile behavior towards them from faculty, and feelings of loneliness. In Bouws et al. (2016), a hermeneutic phenomenological study on lived experience of new nursing deans, the seven study participants, who were all women, also reported being excluded by other university deans, who were male. The deans described their work environments as "highly political", "male-dominated", and "patriarchal" (Bouws et al., 2016, pp. 49-50). Responses from higher-level nursing administrators regarding their experiences with the phenomenon of racism and their perceptions the effects of racism on Black students were highly anticipated as they might have added great value to this dissertation study.

Faculty

Nursing faculty create and manage the teaching and learning environment in nursing schools for aspiring nurses. Nursing faculty prepare nursing students with the knowledge, attitudes, and skills needed to promote health, prevent disease, and provide care to diverse groups of people, across a wide variety of healthcare settings. Faculty prepare students for the workforce (AACN, 2019; Lewis & Bryan, 2021). Nursing faculty are thus practitioners in two distinct disciplines: education and nursing (Booth et al., 2016). Clinical nursing faculty facilitate practical clinical experiences at off-campus sites with clinical agencies such as hospitals, long-term care facilities, and community-based clinics. Academic nurse educators, typically known by the term, "faculty", teach in the college or university (academic) setting. Academic nurse educators may also practice in both the clinical and the academic settings (Fressola & Patterson, 2017). For clarity, the term "nursing faculty" was used in this dissertation study to denote both academic and clinical faculty, with a particular emphasis on academic nurse educators. The term, "clinical faculty" was used to specify educators who only teach in the clinical setting. The roles of academic nurse educators, were delineated into eight core competencies by the National League for Nursing (NLN):

> (1) facilitate learning, (2) facilitate learner development and socialization, (3) use assessment and evaluation strategies, (4) participate in curriculum design and evaluation of program outcomes, (5) function as a change agent and leader, (6) pursue continuous quality improvement in the nurse educator role, (7) engage in scholarship, and (8) function within the educational environment (Fressola & Patterson, 2017, pp. 18-23; National League for Nursing [NLN] Cert. Comm., 2012 as cited in Fitzgerald et al., 2020, p. 5).

In a similar vein, and pertinent to this study's two research questions which focus on perception and attribution of meaning, Rogers et al. (2020) conducted an integrative literature review of articles which identified essential elements of nursing faculty orientations in which they addressed strategies for facilitating the transition from clinical nursing to the academic expectations of teaching, scholarship, and service. The Rogers et al. (2020) study merits a brief discussion here as it adds a realistic view of how nursing faculty apply the core competencies listed above. Faculty at most universities are expected to fulfill teaching, scholarship, and service obligations. The service obligation, for example, might equate to the NLN core competency of "function[ing] within the educational environment" (NLN Cert. Comm., 2012 as cited in Fitzgerald et al., 2020, p. 5) and requires serving within the department, school, or college; serving within the university; serving within the community outside of the institution; and maintaining a professional nursing practice. Nurses in the articles reviewed by Rogers et al. (2020) were oriented to teaching requirements such as familiarization with learning management systems, navigating library reserves and information technology requests, understanding the curriculum, evaluating student learning, and in some cases, receiving preparation in pedagogy (Rogers et al., 2020). Not all nursing educators received formal educational preparation for teaching in their graduate programs (Booth et al., 2016). To fulfill the scholarship requirement, faculty may have to produce a certain number of scholarly publications, presentations and grants for tenure and promotion (Rogers et al., 2020).

Understanding not only faculty roles but also the complexity of the transition from clinical nurse to academic nurse educator is important to this exploration of nursing educators' understanding of the meaning of racism and its effects on Black students. What is significant to this discussion about nursing faculty roles and preparation for those roles is that which is absent from the Rogers et al. (2020) article and not always explicitly stated in other articles describing the nursing faculty role: Nursing faculty must also be oriented to the task of creating inclusive teaching learning environments (Dewsbury, 2022). Fressola and Patterson (2017) introduced nursing educators to useful, specific strategies for "dealing with a diverse student population" in a comprehensive book targeting master's-prepared nurses and clinical faculty entering academia (Fressola & Patterson, 2017, p. 89). *Transition From Clinician to Educator: A Practical Approach* covered topics of relevance for clinicians transitioning to academia, such as teaching in the classroom and the clinical setting, evaluation techniques, curriculum development, integrating technology into nursing education, tenure and promotion, and accreditation. Fressola and Patterson's (2017) recommended approaches to "diversity in the classroom" for nurses transitioning from clinical practice to the academic setting included the following: to "be unbiased", "take advantage of the rich cultural diversity in the classroom" when assigning students to groups, "monitor students' commentaries" and "remain aware of undertones during discussions" in order to interject and defuse attacks when necessary, and to "keep an open mind free of preconceived ideas and biases" (Fressola & Patterson, 2017, p. 89). They warned against ignoring the individuality of "minority" students by making assumptions related to a collective group identity (Fressola & Patterson, 2017, p. 89). Other nursing education scholars such as Akamine Phillips et al. (2019), Dillard-Wright et al. (2023), Iheduru-Anderson and Wahi (2022), and Sumpter et al. (2023) could be seen to agree with the need for faculty to be aware of what is being said and to intervene, when necessary, during classroom discussions. They would further contend that nursing faculty should also be proactive in ending the silence on racism and add teaching antiracism to nursing curricula. The discussion on teaching antiracism continues later in this chapter.

The next two sections handle nursing knowledge and its application to nursing education and are related to nursing faculty practices. Depending upon the teaching philosophy to which one subscribes, nursing faculty teaching practices might be teacher-centered or learner-centered. In a scholarly article outlining teachers' roles and strategies, Horsfall et al. (2012) described teacher-centered teaching as a traditional form of pedagogy in which content, recall, and skill acquisition are emphasized. Knowledge is acquired "predominately from positivist, factual, concrete, technical, and rational forms of knowledge with individual behavioural, cognitive, and/or psychomotor skills (measurable) outcomes" (Horsfall et al., 2012, p. 930). The teacher is assumed to be the subject expert who transmits knowledge to the student. With this approach, the teacher is expected to provide the student with as much of the most current data on the subject possible. Learner-centered teaching is described as more contemporary method than teacher-centered, and the process of learning is considered as important as the content of the teaching. This method draws the learner into the process of learning as an active participant, encourages interaction between teacher and learners, and requires learners to think critically and make decisions about difficult topics. "There is a particular emphasis on dialogue and interpretation of information from a variety of perspectives" (Horsfall et al., 2012, p. 930). Learner-centered teaching is "characterized by an awareness and amelioration of power differences between students and teachers" (Horsfall et al., 2012, p. 931). Acknowledgement of power differences in the nursing classroom is significant to this dissertation study's RQ2. An understanding of nursing faculty's approach to teaching is significant to a discussion about practices that include or exclude Black nursing students. The knowledge that nursing faculty impart upon their nursing students and how they impart that knowledge or mutually discover knowledge with their students affects student outcomes, including future clinical nursing practice and professional identity. Regardless of teaching styles, per Fressola and Patterson (2017), nursing faculty is responsible for assuring that students learn in their classes.

Knowledge Basis for Clinical Nursing Practice

Most nurses that teach nursing have had clinical experience as practicing nurses. Nursing faculty teach what they know, and they often teach the way they were taught (Boswell & Cannon, 2016b; Horsfall et al., 2012; Sumpter et al., 2023). They teach their students to use evidence-based clinical practices (Boswell & Cannon, 2016b). Nursing faculty are typically well-versed on the meanings and implications of evidence-based practice (EBP) because EBP has been a standard in healthcare and a foundation of nursing practice for several years (Booth et al., 2016; Boswell & Cannon, 2016b). Evidence-based practices have predominated nursing education since their adoption by nursing in the 1990s. Evidence-based practice in nursing followed a movement in medicine in the 1990s calling for practitioners to replace knowledge, instinct, and past experience with formally codified clinical decision-making processes based on empirical evidence (Nelson, 2014). Evidence-based practices (EBP) are practices based on scientific research that has been published in current, peer-reviewed literature, and which provide guidelines for implementation (Nelson, 2014). Empiric evidence from quantitative studies involving "data-based, experimental, and quasi-experimental research methodologies" (Chinn et al., 2022, p. 45) has traditionally been considered the more credible and reliable evidence for transfer to clinical practice than knowledge obtained through qualitative studies. Evidence-based practice "emphasizes the use of the strongest level of evidence possible in making clinical decisions and downplays other factors important in the decision-making process" (Nelson, 2014, p. 1514).

Chinn et al. (2022) contended, in *Knowledge Development in Nursing: Theory and Process* (11th ed.), that nursing decision-making should be "evidence-informed" (Chinn et al., 2022, pp. 45, 217), with consideration for multiple forms of knowledge; not just empirical evidence from research. Evidence-informed knowledge is derived from research, clinical circumstances, patient preferences, and expert practitioner opinion. Evidence-informed practices may be thought of as the integration of research-based evidence and best practices that center on the patient (Chinn et al., 2022). The concept of "best practice" originated in the industrial sector of business and was associated with process improvement. Best practices in nursing are typically evidence-based practices employed by nurses, supported by institutions, and favorable from the perspective of patients and their family members because they produce favorable outcomes to those constituents (Nelson, 2014). Best practices are "generally accepted, standardized techniques, methods or processes that have proven themselves over time" (Moore, 2019, para. 4) and are not always based on empirical evidence. Best practices are derived from multiple types of evidence (Nelson, 2014; ten Ham-Baloyi et al., 2020).

Evidence-based Teaching Practices (EBTP) and Innovation

While nursing faculty teach their students the use of evidence-based clinical practices, it is unclear whether faculty practice evidence-based teaching. There is limited evidence in the literature of nursing faculty's understanding and adoption of evidence-based teaching strategies (EBTS) (Boswell & Cannon, 2016b; Culyer et al., 2018; Kalb et al., 2015). Perhaps this is due to most nursing faculty not having received formal education in nursing education (Fitzgerald et al., 2020). Boswell and Cannon (2016a) encouraged nursing educators to apply the same approach to educational practices that nurses apply to clinical practices. Their book, *Evidence-Based Teaching In Nursing: A Foundation for Educators* (2nd ed) includes rationale to support current and recommended teaching strategies. Boswell and Cannon (2016b) based their definition of evidence-based teaching (EBT) in nursing partly on Emerson and Records' (2008) advice that all roles in nursing education (staff, faculty, administrator) are responsible for "the validation, generation, application, and perpetuation of those methods that facilitate the preparation of skilled and thoughtful nurses" (Emerson & Records, 2008, p. 361). Emerson and Records (2008) stated, in a literature review on the scholarship of nursing education, that their definition of EBT was a vision for the future of nursing and was subject to expansion. They advised nursing educators to look outside of nursing to other disciplines for evidence-based teaching practices and to take risks to embrace new technologies and develop new educational strategies. Almost a decade after Emerson and Records' (2008) publication, Boswell and Cannon (2016a) stated that they searched the literature and found no models of ways to implement evidence-based teaching strategies (EBTS).

Culyer et al. (2018) explored nursing faculty's ability to facilitate the transfer of knowledge from theory to practice and found evidence of the use of EBTS. Evidence-based teaching strategies used most often by participants in the Culyer et al. (2018) study included simulation, reflection, small groups, case-based learning, and problem-based learning. They found that faculty's confidence in the effectiveness of EBTS positively influenced faculty's use of EBTS. Pre-licensure nursing faculty surveyed for the Culyer et al. (2018) study described an institutional culture of support as a facilitator for using evidence-based teaching strategies (EBTS). Faculty in cultures of support had available resources such as classrooms equipped with technology and simulation facilitators, as well as supportive administrative leadership and students who were motivated to learn. Cultures with a lack of support for EBTS lacked technology, supplies, faculty development, time, and motivated students (Culyer et al., 2018). There are not many other exemplars documented in nursing education literature of implementation of EBTS. Nursing faculty may be employing EBTS teaching strategies that yield great results for their students and not be publishing their work, thereby neglecting the scholarship of transmitting those practices into evidence-based teaching practices (Kalb et al., 2015; Moore, 2019; Patterson & Klein, 2012).

Understanding the culture in which nursing educators practice is as essential to this dissertation study as is understanding nursing education scholarship and how nursing educators acquire and disseminate knowledge. Dzurec (2022) discussed workplace culture in nursing education as a possible deterrent to adopting evidence-based teaching practices. In contrast to the

Culyer et al. (2018) mixed method descriptive study surveying 166 participants, Dzurec's (2022) used a narrative analysis methodology to conduct qualitative interviews with 19 participants. Nursing faculty shared how the culture in their workplaces discouraged creative thinking and innovative teaching. Novice nurse educators reflected on being passively socialized into the role of faculty by their peers through the various types of stories told about the nature of the work. An example of discouraging narratives was that nursing curricula was very specific and needed to be taught a certain way to prepare students for "high-stakes testing" (Dzurec, 2022, p. 7). Another story told was that if the nursing program was highly successful, there was a "we have arrived" sentiment (Dzurec, 2022, p. 7). Novel ways of teaching were thought to be unnecessary and would not be accepted by peers. Dzurec (2022) labeled the culture of storytelling which discouraged innovation a culture of bullying. She recommended that administrators take action to ensure a safe, supportive workplace culture that addresses diversity and support for fellow faculty and that includes "socialization and celebration" (Dzurec, 2022, p. 7). Patterson and Klein (2012) also emphasized action related to EBTP. They called for a shift from discussing EBTP to taking action to support the creation and dissemination of research on best practices in nursing education. Kalb et al. (2015) recommended a systematic approach to implementing and sharing EBTPs.

Using Emerging Technology

Nursing educators' adoption of emerging technology is considered here as an exemplar of nursing education practices (Culyer et al., 2018). One of the premises of this dissertation study was that explicating current nursing education practices around adoption of new ways of thinking about knowledge and technology may shed light on the lived experience of being a nursing educator. Studies published around pandemic teaching and learning practices emphasized the positive disruptive opportunities the COVID-19 pandemic presented to nursing education (Kativhu, 2021). Prior to the pandemic, the American Association of Colleges of Nursing (AACN) (2019) urged nursing academics to critically examine and reconsider approaches to nursing education. The AACN envisioned, "Nurse educators…nimble enough to embrace new technology and explore fresh approaches to teaching designed to satisfy the diverse learning needs of contemporary nursing students" (AACN, 2019, p. 3). When faculty and students shifted from in-person to remote teaching during the pandemic, many nursing faculty learned to use new technology (Li et al., 2022; Nurse-Clark & Joseph, 2022; Weberg et al., 2021). Faculty embraced new technology out of necessity and, eventually, convenience. Evidence points to nursing educators' implementing technology for teaching and to the ongoing need to adapt nursing programs to life after the pandemic (Leaver et al., 2022).

Among the "fresh approaches" the AACN (2019) recommended be considered by nursing programs were increased emphasis on faculty development, attention to adult learning styles, advancement of diversity, equity, inclusion and belonging (DEIB) efforts, and promotion of active and adaptive learning that utilizes emerging technology (AACN, 2019). In the qualitative research conducted in this research study, the themes formulated in RQ1 and RQ2 aimed to explore whether similar learning is or has been part of the lived experience of nursing educators at PWIs.

Active & Inclusive Teaching and Learning

Several authors gave recommendations for nursing educators to create active, inclusive teaching learning environments. Lewis and Bryan (2021) described andragogy, or adult learning theories of active learning and constructivism. Active learning engages students directly with challenging activities that build their capacity for critical thinking and problem-solving.

Constructivism purports that the adult learner brings existing experiences to the educational setting upon which to build by looking critically at new experiences, and it places the adult learner at the center of the educational experience (Lewis & Bryan, 2021). Concept-based learning is a method of constructivist teaching offered by Lewis and Bryan (2021). Concept-based learning allows students to focus on broad concepts across various settings and times in their education. Relating to smaller parts of concepts, or exemplars, helps students with understanding concepts.

Dewsbury et al. (2022) recommended interrupted lecture with formative questions and "flipped" classrooms with no lectures. Reflection, simulation, and unfolding case studies were discussed by Culyer et al. (2018), and Rao (2019) suggested using debate as an active teaching strategy. With simulation, students can practice clinical skills in safe, controlled environments where they can interact with the educators. Educators are expected to debrief students during or after simulation activities to encourage critical reflection and to build students' confidence with problem solving and communication (Aebersold, 2018; Ghasemi et al., 2020). Case-based learning uses complex, realistic scenarios to promote critical thinking and clinical decision-making (Rao, 2019). Case studies can be effective when educators have students work together in small groups. The process of unfolding case studies requires educators to build on clinical scenarios over the course of time and allows students both to build on previous knowledge and to construct new knowledge (Culyer et al., 2018). Flipped classrooms encourage self-directed learning. In a flipped classroom, students teach themselves the material that the educator would have otherwise presented in class, prior to class. During class time, faculty engages students, encouraging them to assess their knowledge through activities such as discussion of the material, case-studies, and quizzes (Lewis & Bryan, 2021). Debate as a teaching strategy requires students to research both sides and multiple aspects of an argument. It challenges students' beliefs and pre-conceived notions and develops teamwork, communication skills, and critical thinking skills (Lewis & Bryan, 2021; Rao, 2019). Reflection entails a critical examination of an experience and of one's feelings and responses around an experience. Reflection assists the student to develop self-awareness and self-regulation (Bjerkvik & Hilli, 2019). Lewis and Bryan (2021) gave examples of how active teaching strategies were used in their classrooms and of their students' responses. They reported that their students believed the active learning strategies were beneficial and enhanced learning (Lewis & Bryan, 2021). Student-centered teaching is a departure from traditional, linear formats of transferring nursing knowledge, such as lecturing, and it is an inclusive practice (Culyer et al., 2018; Lewis & Bryan, 2021).

Dewsbury et al. (2022) distinguished active learning and inclusive teaching. Active learning involved moving away from the traditional, passive, and unidirectional ways of teaching - which centered on the teacher lecturing for most of the class, over-using slide presentations, and assessing students' attainment of course objectives with a few summative evaluations—to an approach where students were engaged in learning through small group activities and multiple formative evaluation opportunities that counted towards their final grade. Inclusive teaching required the teacher to listen to students by engaging them in dialogue, or "deep teaching" (Dewsbury et al., 2022, p. 4). Creating an inclusive teaching space required teachers to first acknowledge their own biases and suppositions, then develop an understanding of the "psychosocial contexts" (Dewsbury et al., 2022, p. 4) students brought to the classroom. Dewsbury et al. (2022) documented evidence, over a five-year period, that when inclusive, student-centered, active-learning approaches were implemented, the academic performance and outcomes of Black students in STEM courses at a Predominately White Institution (PWI) were greatly improved. They found differences in performance among ethnic groups between sections where the teacher employed inclusive teaching and active learning strategies and sections where the teacher used traditional, passive teaching methods. Inclusive approaches significantly narrowed the achievement gap between Black students and White students in the Dewsbury et al. (2022) study.

Are These Strategies Being Implemented in Nursing Education?

Because much of nursing education scholarship has been focused on clinical skills and practice (Iheduru-Anderson & Alexander, 2022), it is not clear the extent to which the active and inclusive teaching and learning strategies described above are being used. Booth et al. (2016) gave context for the practice of prioritizing clinical research over nursing education science in their explanation of the preparation of the academic nurse educator. They chronicled the history of nursing graduate education over the past 40 to 50 years and its shift from advancing nursing leadership in education and administration to producing advanced clinical practitioners. Poor preparation for the academic nurse educator role may contribute to nursing educators' inadequate documentation of evidence-based inclusive teaching practices. While it is expected that nursing faculty have graduate-level academic preparation and expertise in a clinical specialty, not all nurses who take on faculty roles learn the science of teaching and education in their graduate programs (Booth et al., 2016).

Lewis and Bryan (2021) identified as the research problem of their study that novice nursing educators at their institution were unfamiliar with the theoretical frameworks and teaching techniques that supported the curriculum. The *AACN's Vision for Academic Nursing* (2019) spells out the problem of preparation for the role of nursing faculty: "the major articulated faculty competence is practice specialization within the discipline rather than the process of teaching" (AACN, 2019, p. 13). Perhaps there is not a plethora of nursing educators who are documenting implementation of evidence-based teaching practices because many nursing educators are not sufficiently prepared academically for the specialties of teaching nursing and nursing education scholarship.

Insufficient documentation of inclusive teaching practices is not unique to nursing. Evidence was not clearly delineated throughout STEM higher education in general until recently (Dewsbury et al., 2022). Higher education has lagged behind K-12 education in documenting evidence of inclusive practices in the classroom that positively affect the outcomes of "historically disenfranchised" students (Dewsbury et al., 2022). The Sumpter et al. (2023) integrative review is one study by nursing educators that gathered evidence of inclusive teaching strategies from other disciplines. Sumpter et al. (2023) is reviewed further later in this chapter in the section on Nursing Curriculum: Teaching Anti-Racism. A discussion around the gap in evidence of nursing educators' inclusive teaching practices aligns with this study's RQ2 and justified this qualitative phenomenological study on nursing faculty's understandings of the effects of racism on Black nursing students.

Eliminating Gaps

Academically, nursing faculty play pivotal roles in helping or hindering students to make the connections between theory and practice needed to practice professionally. Students in the Henderson et al. (2020) study considered faculty to be a bridge during the transition from being students to practicing professionally as nurses. See et al. (2023) reported that nurses graduating and starting work during the pandemic were unhappy with their work because of the "dissonance between their academic training and actual nursing practice" (See et al., 2023, p. 9). Disparities between what students learn in the educational setting and what they need to know in the employment setting are known, collectively, as a preparation to practice gap (Kavanagh &

Sharpnack, 2021). Nursing educators must be aware that, in addition to their task of narrowing

the gap between what students learn in nursing school and what they are expected to be able to

do in the workplace (Culyer et al., 2018), they are also responsible for eliminating the academic

achievement gap that may exist between White students and students from historically

disenfranchised groups (Dewsbury et al., 2022). Another role of nursing educators is socializing

nursing students into the profession and the culture of nursing (Salisu et al., 2019).

Socialization into Nursing

Socialization is immersion into the culture of nursing. Socialization "is a process that

begins with getting acquainted with the professional roles and gaining a professional identity"

(Salisu et al., 2019, p. 1289). Socialization into the profession is inevitable. Unfortunately, not all

educators realize their role in "[instilling] professional values and attitudes in neophytes" (Salisu

et al., 2019, p. 1289). Fitzgerald et al. (2020) found that nursing educators in their study fell short

of the NLN's *Core Competencies for Nurse Educators* in the area of socializing nursing students

into the professional nursing role. In addition to spending time with peers, working in teams, and

building professional and personal relationships, socialization also involves quality interactions

with nursing educators. Communication, mentoring, expectation-setting, and role modeling from

supportive educators teach nursing students the values, behaviors, and expectations of

professional nursing. Students who are sufficiently socialized into the profession have the

confidence and motivation to succeed in the nursing profession (Salisu et al., 2019). On the

other hand, students with insufficient professional socialization because of factors such as social

isolation, lack of role models, and microaggressions are at risk for dissatisfaction with nursing

and for dropping out of nursing school (Matthews et al., 2022). Bell (2021) cautioned that socialization reproduces "problematic values, ideals and culture, unless intentionally interrupted" (Bell, 2021, p. 3).

Current scholarship on faculty and administrator roles and on the inclusion of staff in strategic planning gives insight into nursing educators' direct influence on the social and emotional well-being of nursing students. Nursing educators' caring behaviors have a profound influence on students' experience in nursing school and on their intent to graduate. Henderson et al. (2020) conducted a systemic review of literature published in various countries between 2014 and 2019. Data synthesized from 10 studies related to nursing student attrition and graduation and faculty incivility and support showed that nursing faculty's display of caring and empathy towards nursing students was perceived by students as a factor affecting a sense of belonging in nursing school and intent to graduate.

Nursing Curriculum

Whiteness and Colorblindness

The cultural and racial diversity of the United States is not well represented by nursing educators overall (Green, 2020). Nursing education continues to be a "non-inclusive environment" (Bell, 2021, p. 3) with curricula that reproduces "dominant norms such as Whiteness, heteronormativity, middle and upper-classism and positivism" (Bell, 2021, p. 3). Whiteness in nursing curricula manifests through practices such as presenting race as a biological rather than a social construct (Bell, 2021; Idehuru-Anderson & Alexander, 2022), centering healthiness on White skin tones, excluding photos of healthy people of color in textbooks and presentations, and not teaching about the history and contributions of nurses of color (Idehuru-Anderson & Alexander, 2022).

In addition to being predominately White, more than half of today's nursing faculty and administrators are over the age of 45 (NLN, 2022a), likely having attended nursing school several years ago, and having become nurses in spaces where the curricula was centered on Whiteness; spaces where there was power and privilege in Whiteness and anything or anyone outside of that norm was different or relegated to "otherness" (Iheduru-Anderson & Alexander, 2022; Puzan, 2003; White & Fulton, 2015). Nursing educators whose own professional nursing identity was developed in Whiteness often will not recognize, on their own, the divide between them and their Black students unless that information is expressly brought to their attention (Puzan, 2003).

Bell's (2021) literature review found that educators in some settings actively resisted acknowledging issues around racism and the need for teaching anti-racism (Bell, 2021). Ohito (2016) used the fairy tale, *The Emperor's New Clothes* to illustrate ignorance as a choice to refuse to receive knowledge that challenges one's perceptions of oneself. In the fairy tale, an emperor paraded through town pretending to wear the new suit crafted for him out of invisible material by a tailor that had duped the emperor. The townspeople went along with the emperor's delusion and praised his new suit as he passed them by. A young child proclaimed that the emperor was, in fact, unclothed. Rather than acknowledge that the boy was correct: there was no suit and that he was naked in front of all the townspeople, "the emperor chooses to keep moving along, rejecting the knowledge that he is naked, thus illustrating that ignorance is not a passive lack of knowledge, but an active detachment from that which we do not want to know (Ohito, 2016, p. 455). Against this backdrop, the significance of this research study's questions become amplified; anti-racist teaching and learning are imperatives that need to be addressed in nursing education and practice (Ackerman-Barger & Hummel, 2015; Blanchet Garneau et al., 2018; Iheduru-Anderson & Alexander, 2022; Iheduru-Anderson & Waite, 2022).

Sawyer and Waite (2021) argued in their special report addressing social justice and equity in higher education that in the U.S. it is generally understood that the only validated experience and narrative is the White experience and narrative. Sawyer and Waite (2021) defined Whiteness as a "position of structural advantage in race privilege" (Sawyer & Waite, 2021, p. 3). White healthcare workers have not been equipped to adequately address the public health issue of racism because they were socialized to be ignorant of racism and of the history of racism (Dancis & Coleman, 2022). Nursing educators play a major role in that system as they are part of and prepare the largest portion of the healthcare workforce (Iheduru-Anderson & Alexander, 2022). Nursing educators' lack of understanding, or ignorance of, the unique needs of their Black students may reinforce biases and contribute to discrimination these students (Wesp et al., 2018). Dancis and Coleman (2022) framed their study teaching antiracism on the theory of White epistemology of ignorance. Mills (2007) described this lack of knowledge, among White people, about racism, its history, its normalcy, and its effects on society as White ignorance. Ignorance about racism significantly contributes to health inequities and overt discrimination (Wesp et al., 2018). Bell (2021) describes this ignorance as a "lack of perspective that comes with lived experience" (Bell, 2021, p. 3). Bell (2021) further stated that when nursing education leadership positions are occupied by "homogenous" groups, the lack of perspective about race and racism is reflected in the both the explicit and the null curricula. Approaching nursing education from a culturalist perspective by teaching "cultural competency", "cultural sensitivity" and "culturally congruent care" (Blanchet Garneau et al., 2018, p. 2) ignores the role of racism as a causative factor of social and health inequities. Instructing nursing students about differences based on culture and racialized identity reflects ignorance and colorblindness and is embedded in the implicit or hidden curriculum of nursing (Bell, 2021; Blanchet Garneau et al., 2018; Iheduru-Anderson & Alexander, 2022).The hidden curriculum was defined by Iheduru-Anderson and Alexander (2022) as "a learning dimension of culturally acquired, unintended lessons that are considered common sense and cannot be quantified or evaluated. Students are socialized for professional roles through the hidden curriculum" (Iheduru-Anderson & Alexander, 2022, p. 8).

Teaching Cultural Competency

Cultural competency has been taught in nursing for decades, (Davis & O'Brien, 2020; Iheduru-Anderson & Alexander, 2022). Cultural competency is supposedly achieved by studying a specific culture with the goal of obtaining a set of instructions on how to work with people of that culture (Wesp et al., 2018). Cultural competency is considered a skill in nursing and is referred to as nurses' capacity to care for diverse patient populations. According to Davis and O'Brien (2020), cultural competency "largely focuses on communication skills and linguistic strategies to address culturally specific sources of stigma" (Davis & O'Brien, 2020, p. S60). Cultural competency, as expressed by Adeniran et al. (2023), is nurses' knowledge of, or willingness to become knowledgeable of, the culture of the patient. In its current state in nursing education, cultural competency is ill-defined, uncodified, and immeasurable (Iheduru-Anderson & Alexander, 2022). Cultural competency, in Iheduru-Anderson and Alexander's (2022) view, has never been integrated into nursing education to the point of being formally evaluated as a competency for nursing students. Adeniran et al. (2023) found that many of the nurses they surveyed could not define cultural competence, were not taught it in school, and had no mandate to practice it in their workplaces. Many of the nursing faculty in the Chen et al. (2020) study were not well-equipped to teach their students to be culturally competent, as they were not culturally competent themselves.

Bell (2021) searched multidisciplinary literature on anti-racism, Whiteness, and privilege in nursing education and analyzed 41 articles. She found much criticism in the literature of nursing education's "complicity in delivering politically soft curricula" (Bell, 2021, p. 3). Outstanding criticisms of nursing education in Bell's (2021) report were that colorblindness and "equal treatment ideology" prevented understanding of racism and social disparities, and the "tenaciously predominant culturalist approach to nursing across difference" (Bell, 2021, p.3) ignored race and racism and normalized Eurocentrism. Bell's (2021) review of the literature was comprehensive, essentially charging nursing educators with being silent on racism and lacking the critical awareness and competence to deliver content that has "anti-racist, anti-discriminatory, post-colonial and intersectional perspectives" (Bell, 2021, p. 9). According to Ackerman-Barger & Hummel (2015), the acquisition of cultural competency assumes the person acquiring the skill holds a certain position of privilege and power over another individual or group. Iheduru-Anderson and Waite's (2022) appraisal of the inclusion of cultural competency in nursing curriculum is that it emphasizes "power dynamics and perceiving non-Whites as 'other'", and "validates assumed inferiority of the marginalized group" (Iheduru-Anderson & Waite, 2022, p. 2).

Nursing curriculum has historically relegated teaching anti-racism to the null curriculum and emphasized teaching cultural competency. In doing so, nursing education has masked "a system of White dominance and privilege in nursing education" and "created the illusion of equity and inclusion" (Ackerman-Barger & Hummel, 2015, p. 45). Wesp et al. (2018) advocated for "an emancipatory approach to cultural competency, informed by the theories of postcolonial feminism, intersectionality theory, and critical race theory" (p. 322). Their arguments against the "Guidelines for Implementing Culturally Competent Nursing Care" (Douglas et al., 2014) published by the Transcultural Nursing Society (Transcultural Nursing Society, 2014), and widely cited in nursing academia, were many. Wesp et al. (2018) argued that nurses studying a specific culture with the goal of obtaining a set of instructions on how to work with people of that culture is essentializing. That is to say, teaching cultural competency perpetuates the fallacy that culture is static and encourages stereotyping by lumping people together by group affiliation. Wesp et al. (2018) recommended considering individuals and their group affiliations and life experiences without making assumptions. Instead of requiring nurses to learn about providing "culturally congruent care" (Wesp et al., 2018, p. 322), nurses should learn about intersectionality of identities and the structures and processes of power responsible for marginalizing people. The guideline which called for nurses to take an honest assessment of their own culture and biases to understand how they might conflict with their patients' culture and values was viewed through a CRT lens. Wesp et al. (2018) cautioned that one could not truly confront one's own or someone else's biases without a thorough understanding of racism and the language to discuss it. Emancipatory interventions recommended included conversations and interventions, but the specific instructions for implementation were not explicitly stated in the article. Davis and O'Brien (2020) believed that a paradigm shift is occurring, one in which providers move away from focusing on individual patients and their cultures towards

> the lens of structural competency, wherein providers not only recognize the systems, institutional norms, practices, and policies that produce unjust health situations and conditions but also engage in an ongoing process of learning, self-reflection,

collaboration, and advocacy to address the multifaceted social and structural determinants of health disparities, inequities, and outcomes (Davis & O'Brien, 2020, p. S58).

Bell (2021) said that "the tenaciously predominant culturalist approach to nursing across difference" (Bell, 2021, p. 3) is Eurocentric and places nursing students in a space separate from the "other people who have something called culture" (Bell, 2021, p. 3) that they must learn about in nursing school. "Cultural competence", "culturally congruent care", and "multiculturism" are terms used alongside "culture", "ethnicity", and "diversity", often to signify race. As currently taught in nursing education, cultural competence fails to address the social determinants of health rooted in systemic and structural of racism in the U.S. (Bell, 2021; Blanchet Garneau et al., 2018; Wesp et al., 2018).

Anti-racist Education

Alongside teaching cultural competence, Iheduru-Anderson and Alexander (2022) promoted anti-racist education. Several other writers advocated for the inclusion of emancipatory, anti-discriminatory, anti-oppressive, or anti-racist teaching in nursing education (Bell, 2021; Dancis & Coleman, 2022; Blanchet Garneau et al., 2018; Iheduru-Anderson & Waite, 2022; Sumpter et al., 2023; Wesp et al., 2018). Matthews et al. (2022) called for all nursing institutions to "condemn anti-Black racism" (p. 101). Studies by Sumpter et al. (2023) and Dancis and Coleman (2022) around teaching anti-racism are reviewed here.

Sumpter et al. (2023) conducted an integrative review of literature from multiple disciplines to compile a set of evidence-based strategies for antiracist teaching in nursing. The 18 disciplines represented included education, social work, feminist studies, English, nursing, and medicine. Four themes emerged from the study as teaching strategies: encounter, reflection, discussion, and activism. Encounter strategies involved faculty-facilitated "encounters with the lived experiences of minoritized individuals" (Sumpter et al., 2023, p. 275) that engaged students with antiracist content. Encounters manifested in the form of curricula updated with course materials by authors of color, classroom discussions around films and social media content, reading fictional literature, and exploring emotions that emerged in association with field trips to various communities where the influence of segregation was apparent. Reflection strategies reported in the articles were sometimes "anonymous and ungraded to promote candor and disclosure" (Sumpter et al., 2023) and took many forms, such as written, verbal, blogs, individual or paired work, and focused on affective and emotional learning. Discussion strategies also took many forms and produced various results among students, as far as preferences. The most commonly reported strategy for discussion in antiracist teaching was dividing students into small groups. Activism strategies reported in articles reviewed by Sumpter et al. (2023) varied by students' levels. Graduate students were encouraged by faculty to advocate in the community and engaged in activities such as attending a local school board meeting. Activism for undergraduate students encouraged student empowerment by positioning students as decision-makers and owners of their own learning evaluation methods. The Sumpter et al. (2023) study report concluded by correlating antiracist teaching strategies employed in other disciplines with opportunities for transformative learning experiences through experiential learning in nursing education. "Experiential learning is a cornerstone of nursing education, and our findings indicate experiential strategies prove useful in providing entry points to conversations and teachable moments regarding racism" (Sumpter et al., 2023, p. 277).

Dancis and Coleman (2022) used a "Revealing Systemic Racism" map with nine tabs labeled "gentrification & residential segregation, police brutality, erasure & dehumanization, White supremacy (other tabs not named in the report)" (Dancis & Coleman, 2022, p. 4) and "invoke[d] personal crises" (Dancis & Coleman, 2022, p. 3) for White students, by having students click on places in the tab where students could read and write and discuss how those places related to systemic racism. Dancis and Coleman (2022) challenged White students enrolled in a required equity and diversity course in an RN-to-BSN program to "concretize the abstract concept of systemic racism through place-based learning" (Dancis & Coleman, 2022, p. 5). Students were asked to identify places that represented systemic racism on maps of locations with which they had a personal connection. Part of the assignment was to explain their choices and reflect upon their experiences with the assignment. Dancis and Coleman (2022) reported that students in the study were confronted with their own ignorance of historical and current policies that perpetuated racial disparities, such as real estate redlining and intentionally providing drinking water from contaminated sources to Black communities. Dancis and Coleman (2022) argued that these "transformative dissonant encounters" (Dancis and Coleman, 2022. p. 3) confronted White nursing students' color-blindness and racial innocence and created opportunities for "White people to reframe racism as a social process in which they are personally and collectively implicated" (Dancis & Coleman, 2022, p. 3). Promoting these nursing education researchers' orientation towards disrupting racism by their acknowledging the existence of racism in nursing curriculum and teaching antiracism emphasizes the appropriateness of applying Critical Race Theory (CRT) as a theoretical framework for this dissertation study. "Critical Race Theory argues for the eradication of racial subjugation while simultaneously recognizing that race is a social construct" (Creswell & Poth, 2018, p. 30).

Theoretical Framework: Critical Race Theory

Critical Race Theory (CRT) is misunderstood by many Americans and has been maligned in the news media since Donald Trump decided to attack CRT, labeling it as racist and using his ill-informed categorization of the movement to fuel a growing campaign to remove references to slavery and other aspects of America's racist past from history books (Adams, 2021; Hoadley-Brill, 2024). Critical Race Theory is a scholarly movement that originated within U.S. legal studies in response to the inertia that seemed to have set into the Civil Rights movement after Dr. Martin Luther King, Jr.'s death (Delgado & Stefancic, 2017; Hoadley-Brill, 2024; MSNBC, 2021). The pioneers of CRT were legal scholars of color, studying or teaching in law schools (Crenshaw et al., 1995, Introduction; Khalifa et al., 2013) who left the "Critical Legal Studies" (CLS) workshop (Donnor & Ladson-Billings, 2024, p. 144) to form their own group. Delgado and Stefancic (2017) described CRT as "a collection of activists and scholars engaged in studying and transforming the relationship among race, racism, and power" (Delgado & Stefancic, 2017, p. 3). Kimberlé Crenshaw, one of the originators of the CRT movement, noted that, although early CRT scholars did not all subscribe to the same philosophies or methodologies, they were united by two common goals.

> to understand how a regime of White supremacy and its subordination of people of color have been created and maintained in America, and, in particular, to examine the relationship between that social structure and professed ideals such as "the rule of law" and "equal protection". The second [goal] is a desire not merely to understand the vexed bond between law and racial power but to *change* it (Crenshaw et al., 1995, p. xiii).

Crenshaw described Critical Race Theory (CRT) as a "way of looking at race" (MSNBC, 2021, 2:59). As she explained in an MSNBC news interview with journalist Joy Reid, CRT was a way of telling the stories of the people of color who were subordinated, rather than freed, by the law (MSNBC, 2021). Cornel West called CRT "one set of lenses that looks at America through the lens of those who were enslaved, Jim Crow, Jane Crow, lynched, discriminated against, degraded, debased" (The Divine Names, 2022, 2:23). Derrick Bell described CRT in "Faces at

the Bottom of the Well" as "a new scholarly song" (Bell, 1992, p. 144). Bell (1992) explained

that he and his colleagues had created a new ideology, with components borrowed from

philosophy and the social sciences. The legal scholars that Bell (1992) credited with this creation

were Patricia Williams, Angela Harris, Kimberlé Crenshaw, Mari Matsuda, Richard Delgado,

Gerald Torres, Lani Guinier, and Charles Lawrence (Bell, 1992, p. 144).

Critical Race Theory was born "as a scholarly and politically committed movement"

(West, 1995, p. xi) when Derrick Bell, legal scholar and first Black tenured professor at Harvard

Law School (HLS News Staff, 2011), began to publish his views examining the role of the law in

maintaining a system of social domination and subordination in the U.S. Bell maintained that

civil rights lawyers at the NAACP Legal Defense Fund (LDF) - where he himself administered

hundreds of desegregation cases in the 1960s – were pressured into integrating schools in the

1954 *Brown v. Board of Education* case and "sold out their clients" (Alexander, 2018, p. xv). He

contended that LDF lawyers knew that sending Black children to White schools was a betrayal of

the Black community and would not guarantee a better quality of education for Black children

(Alexander, 2018; Bell, 1995a). Bell continued to explore and expound upon his convictions

through essays and fictional stories like "The Space Traders" (Alexander, 2018; Bell,

1992/2018). Bell's message, and the basic premise of Critical Race Theory, was that racism is

permanent and persistent in this country and will only be mitigated every now and then for the

convenience of White people. "Black interests, he said, will always be sacrificed for White gain"

(Alexander, 2018, p. xvii).

The assertation that racism is normal, "ordinary, not aberrational" (Delgado & Stefancic,

2017, p. 7) is the first of five basic tenets of Critical Race Theory (CRT) (Delgado and Stefancic,

2017; UNCA, 2015). CRT is grounded in the understanding that racism is an everyday occurrence in the United States. The denial of the ordinariness of racism and the looking past discrimination against racialized and marginalized groups of people is known as "colorblindness" (Delgado & Stefancic, 2017, p. 7). Seeing racism as blatant, violent acts of individuals against other individuals, rather than seeing it as structural and systemic, is a form of colorblindness. Treating all people equally and "not seeing color" are also forms of colorblindness. In *Critical Race Theory: The Key Writings that Formed the Movement*, Neil Gotanda examined the U.S. Supreme Court's claim of the colorblindness of the U.S. Constitution, stating that "a color-blind interpretation of the Constitution legitimates and thereby maintains the social, economic, and political advantages that Whites hold over other Americans" (Gotanda, 1995, p. 257). To fully understand colorblindness, it is essential to look back at the history of segregation and constitutional law. That the Constitution was colorblind and that all people were equal under the law was the assertation of Supreme Court Justice John Marshall Harlan, who was the sole dissenting voice in the Plessy v. Ferguson case which upheld Jim Crow segregation in the U.S. Harlan used language to imply that the Constitution was colorblind (Bouie, 2023). His words were echoed by conservative Supreme Court justices in their 2023 decision to overturn affirmative action. In an opinion piece for the New York Times, which was not a peer-reviewed scholarly report, but a timely, if not accurate account of the recent, derisive Supreme Court decision, Bouie argued in 2023 that Justice Harlan's dissent was not anchored in a vision of equality for all people of all races, but in a belief that no matter what the law said, Black people would never be equal in America. Bouie (2023) asserted that Harlan's dissent was more of a defense of White racial dominance and a dismissal of any further reason for the Court to waste its time arguing for the equality of Black people than it was an endorsement of equal rights. Bouie (2023) also stated that Harlan viewed segregation through federal law as unnecessary; state law and society would keep segregation firmly intact. Harlan's dissent was practically forgotten over the years. However, in July 2023, conservative Supreme Court justices revived Harlan's language that "there is no caste here. Our Constitution is colorblind, and neither knows nor tolerates classes among citizens" (Bouie, 2023, para. 3) to strike down affirmative action and outlaw college admissions based on race. The repeal of affirmative action may have implications for nursing education and higher education overall that are yet unknown.

The second tenet of Critical Race Theory, interest convergence, asserts that people with the power to eradicate racism will only do so if the outcome is to their benefit (Delgado & Stefancic, 2017). Derrick Bell (1995b) discussed interest convergence in his essay on *Brown v. Board of Education*. He refused to accept the rationale that the *Brown* decision was about recognizing Black people as worthy of "equal educational opportunities" (Bell, 1995b, p. 5). He contended, instead, that the Brown decision was most beneficial to "those Whites in policymaking positions able to see the economic and political advances at home and abroad that would follow abandonment of segregation" (Bell, 1995a, p. 22). Looking humane to the communist world in the midst of the Cold War by declaring Black children as equal, assuring that Black people would continue to join the military and go to war for the United States, and rebuilding the economy of the South by ending state-sanctioned segregation were the impetuses for the *Brown* decision, according to Bell (1995a).

Race as a social construct, rather than a biological one, is the third tenet of CRT (Delgado & Stefancic, 2017). "Races are categories that society invents, manipulates, or retires when convenient" (Delgado & Stefancic, 2017, p. 9). Race is a social, not a biological, construct. Yet, race is often used by miseducated healthcare professionals to diagnose and treat disease. Race is used as a genetic marker contributing to illness and disease when the root cause lies in social determinants of health such as place of residence, exposure to physical and chemical hazards, and poverty (Dancis & Coleman, 2021; Iheduru-Anderson & Alexander, 2022). Iheduru-Anderson and Alexander (2022) discuss the consideration of race as a disease etiology by some healthcare professionals. Racism— not race—is the root cause of systemic inequities that cause illness to individuals and communities. Inability to walk through one's neighborhood safely for exercise and fresh air, and lack of access to fresh fruits and vegetables within walking distance are two examples of determinants of health related to racism, a by-product of the social construct of race. Racism is responsible for illness, in the form of stress, misdiagnosed pain, missed diagnoses, unexplained treatment options, disrespect and lack of support when dealing with complications and death (Hostetter & Klein, 2018). Nursing education often fails to educate students on the social construct of race and the systemic inequities intrinsic to racism (Iheduru-Anderson & Alexander, 2022). □

The fourth tenet of CRT, differential racialization "deals with how the dominant society racializes different minority groups at different times, in response to shifting needs such as the labor market" (Delgado & Stefancic, 2017, p. 10). An example might be how people from Central America might be welcomed into the U.S. to work in an in-demand agricultural industry one year and vilified as "illegal" or shiftless when that crop loses popularity. Intersectionality, the idea that people are multi-faceted, and their identities could place them in multiple categories, is related to differential racialization (Delgado & Stefancic, 2017). Kimberlé Crenshaw is credited with introducing the term "intersectionality" which involves the various ways race, gender, and class intersected, in her essays on Black women's employment and violence against Black women (Crenshaw, 1995, p. 358).

Basile and Black (2019) described the ways differential racialization and racial commodification have been operationalized historically and how they have recently been experienced by Black students in STEM programs at PWIs. In a look-back on history, Basile and Black (2019) saw that Black people were generously employed as agriculture workers and then factory workers as industry moved from the fields to the cities. Once industries moved out of the cities, Black people were portrayed as lazy criminals and were eventually exploited through laws easing their incarceration to fuel a profitable prison industry. Basile and Black (2019) contended that in STEM higher education, Black students at PWIs may be accepted into STEM programs to bolster enrollment rates and be counted towards certain diversity initiatives. However, many of those students are "weeded out" during introductory STEM courses. Those students who are not weeded out are lured into conformity to the dominant culture by "siren songs of uniqueness", a strategy described by Delgado that places conditions on successful Black students and affords them with limited privileges while fostering divisiveness between them and other members of their racial group (Basile & Black, 2019).

The fifth tenet of CRT claims that in chronicling the human experience, there is a unique voice of color that needs to be heard (Delgado & Stefancic, 2017). Legal storytelling and counternarratives allow for various interpretations of an experience. Derrick Bell used legal storytelling in his dialogues with fictional "lawyer-prophet", Geneva Crenshaw (Bell, 1992, p. ix), in "Faces at the Bottom of the Well" and "And We Are Not Saved" to discuss racism and civil rights (Bell, 2018, p. xxi).

Mobilized by Critical Race Theory and feminist studies, legal storytelling constitutes a specific form of writing about law, a social critique, and an epistemology. Because it describes subjective experiences lived by an embodied narrator, this type of storytelling introduces into legal studies narratives of singular experiences to show how law constructs and reproduces gender and racial hierarchies by describing it effects on particular individuals (Saada, 2021, Abstract).

Factual or fictional accounts may run alongside or counter to mainstream accounts of an experience. These counternarratives might be told as parables or dialogues and they amplify "brown and black" (Delgado & Stefancic, 2017, p. 11) voices that might not otherwise be heard. A narrative about the experience of racism during nursing school told by a Black student at a PWI will be unique to that individual and possibly much different from a narrative told by a White nursing student at the same institution or from that of a Black nursing student at an HBCU. At a PWI, where most nursing students and educators are White, the narratives of the majority of individuals will more than likely omit accounts of racial microaggressions and isolation and exclusion related to racism.

The CRT tenet of narrative was applied to this phenomenological study about racism and nursing education, although the unique shared experiences are those of nursing educators at PWIs who may work with Black students; these are narratives seldom heard in nursing education literature. Viewing this study through a CRT lens kept the Black nursing student in focus for the researcher (Khalifa et al., 2013) while nursing educators gave their narratives around meanings of the lived experience of racism. In documenting the narratives around the phenomenon of racism in this study, "CRT scholarship" as Khalifa et al. (2013) emphasized, "stands to contribute greatly to the field of educational leadership because it directly challenges the ubiquitous claims of the colorblind neutrality assumed in data-driven decision-making" (Khalifa et al., 2013, p. 491). This research study underscores and extends this point, iterating the call to challenge both nursing educational leadership and nursing education research.

In this section, current literature was reviewed which presented an overview of nursing education and the roles of nursing educators. Issues around the nursing shortage, attrition of Black nursing students, microaggressions, and racism were central to an essential discussion of looming gaps in nursing education research especially faculty and students at Predominately White Institutions and their lived experiences with racism. As scholarly studies noted, there is a gap in understanding around inequities faced by Black students. To address these gaps, some research has begun to address the need for change in the way teachers of nursing themselves are trained, how the profession itself promotes Evidence Based Teaching Practices (EBTP), and the need for educators to prepare future nursing professionals with structural competency. Teaching anti-racism was also mentioned here. Included were the arguments of a few leaders in nursing education research for embracing Critical Race Theory (CRT) to create inclusive learning environments for nursing students. Chapter III introduces and discusses the methodology that was used for this study.

Chapter III. Methodology

This chapter discusses the research method and procedures applied to an inquiry about nursing educators at Predominately White Institutions and what the lived experience of racism means to them. The qualitative research approach presented in this chapter was designed to address the problem of the lack of data on nursing educators' understanding of racism and the barriers racism creates for Black students at PWIs that may influence their graduation from nursing school. The research design addressed the study's research questions,

RQ1: What are nursing educators at Predominately White Institutions' (PWIs) meanings of the lived experience of racism? and

RQ2: How do nursing educators at Predominately White Institutions (PWIs) perceive the effects or impact of racism on Black nursing students?

The intent of this research was to gather thick data on individuals' meanings of the lived experience of racism and its effects on Black nursing students to get a "complex, detailed understanding" (Creswell & Poth, 2018) of the problem of insufficient evidence of nursing educators' understanding of racism and the impacts of racism on Black students and move towards finding solutions for the problem. A qualitative research design involves talking directly with people (Creswell & Poth, 2018) and is appropriate for eliciting perceptions and meanings of racism from nursing educators (Tilki et al., 2007).

This chapter discusses the rationale for the research approach, the research design, justification of the site and sample selection, data collection procedures, ethical considerations, data analysis, the role of the researcher, and the methods for determining the trustworthiness of the data. Finally, decisions to determine trustworthiness of data are discussed at the end of the chapter.

Rationale for Research Approach

A qualitative research approach was justified for the purpose of this study (Plano Clark & Creswell, 2015; Creswell & Poth, 2018), which was to gain understanding of the meanings of the phenomenon of racism from multiple nursing educators. A qualitative research approach can be used to discover and describe the experiences of multiple individuals (Plano Clark & Creswell, 2015). Qualitative research designs seek to explore and discover by emphasizing words, their analysis, and their grouping into themes. Quantitative methods would not adequately represent the realities of the respondents (Denzin et al., 2024). A quantitative approach would have limited the amount and depth of data that could be gathered through this study. Allowing respondents to speak freely through qualitative data collection methods may have identified variables related to the problem that were not easily measurable and that could not have been uncovered with quantitative methods (Creswell & Poth, 2018). A qualitative research approach involves selection of participants, data collection, and analysis to develop themes, and a discussion of conclusions about themes (Plano Clark & Creswell, 2015).

Braun et al. (2021) promoted qualitative surveys as a primary data collection method and presented compelling rationale for their use. They recognized that participants' accounts are "always situated, partial and particular to the constraints and possibilities of a particular telling" (Braun et al., 2021, p. 651). That is, the meanings participants share at a given time and place and through a particular format are unique and exclusive to that instance. Online surveys completed by the participants on their own time may yield different information on meanings of racism than face-to-face interviews. For this study on nursing educators and racism, online qualitative surveys were appropriate as a primary means of data collection. Interviews, while more commonly used in qualitative research (Plano Clark & Creswell, 2015) were considered the secondary means of collecting data in this study. Potential participants may not have been easy to engage in-person on the topic of racism (Braun et al., 2021), particularly given the current politicized and polarized social climate in the U.S. in which it seemed that any dialogue hinting at Black people as a group being discriminated against was vilified by extremists (who were increasingly loud and powerful) as being anti-White and racist! It was hoped participants would be willing to share in interviews to add to the depth of meaning obtained from surveys about nursing educators' understanding about racism and its effects on Black students. Participants in interviews were offered a copy of their transcript to validate data gathered from interviews.

Research Design

The design of this research study was qualitative. Qualitative research is designed to "develop an understanding about a central phenomenon" (Plano Clark & Creswell, 2015, p. 333). Types of qualitative research design include narrative, case study, ethnography, historical analysis, and phenomenology (Creswell & Poth, 2018; Plano Clark & Creswell, 2015). Phenomenological research aims to capture, in present time and space, the meanings of experiences as they were and are lived (van Manen, 2023). Because of the dynamic nature of lived experiences, replicability was not a goal of this qualitative, phenomenological research study (Stahl & King, 2020). The researcher's intent was to understand the meanings of the lived experience of racism for nursing educators by gathering, analyzing, and reporting data about their realities, experiences, and perspectives (Plano Clark & Creswell, 2015).

This research design was approached with the ontological philosophical assumption that there are multiple realities, those of the participants and those of the researcher (Creswell & Poth, 2018). A phenomenological qualitative research approach was used to address the research questions posed in this study. Throughout the process of conducting this study, the researcher practiced epoché, bracketing, and being reflexive about her own experience and positionality with the phenomenon.

Phenomenological research is rooted in phenomenology, the branch of philosophy that is heavily influenced by philosophers Edmund Husserl, Martin Heidegger, Maurice Merleau-Ponty, and Jean-Paul Sartre (Creswell & Poth, 2018; Vagle et al., 2024). "Phenomenology is the study of the meaning of lived-through experiences – phenomena, as they appear, reveal, and show themselves, and as they give themselves in our consciousness, before they have even been named, conceptualized, abstracted, and/or theorized" (van Manen, 2023, p. 3). Phenomenological research explores meanings of lived experiences; not the "empirical material that mostly consists of perceptions, opinions, beliefs, views…" (Creswell & Poth, 2018, p. 272) and collects and analyzes "experientially descriptive accounts" (Creswell & Poth, 2018, p. 272). Phenomenology is "a preoccupation with the meaningfulness of human lives" (van Manen, 2023, p. 36). van Manen, a contemporary phenomenologist and educator, presented phenomenology as a practical method for exploring ordinary, everyday life (van Manen, 2023). In hermeneutical phenomenological research, the researcher identifies a topic of interest or concern and discusses and interprets the meanings of the topic as a lived experience. A transcendental or psychological phenomenological inquiry relies more on the participant's description of the phenomenon than on the researcher's interpretation of it. Transcendental phenomenology requires epoché – a suspension of judgement - and bracketing so that the researcher can approach the experiences with wonder and see them as fresh and new throughout the course of the study (Creswell & Poth, 2018). A combination of both hermeneutical and transcendental inquiry were used for this study.

A phenomenological approach to inquiry attempts to find meaning in participants' experiences and to group those common meanings into a phenomenon, or common concept or object of the human experience (Creswell & Poth, 2018). Common philosophical assumptions of phenomenological research are that it is the study of people's lived experiences; that people's views of their lived experiences are conscious; and that the essence of phenomena is the description rather than an analysis of the phenomena (Creswell & Poth, 2018). Typical features of phenomenological research studies are an emphasis on a phenomenon, or a single concept; the exploration of the phenomenon with a group of individuals who have all experienced the phenomenon; and the expectation that the researcher will exercise epoché about what is real for the respondents (Creswell & Poth, 2018). A phenomenological methodology of inquiry was appropriate for this dissertation study as it explored lived experiences of the everyday, "ordinariness" of racism (Delgado & Stefancic, 2017; Donnor & Ladson-Billings, 2024) and the effects of racism on Black students from the perspectives of nursing educators, many of whom are White.

Steps for conducting phenomenological research are described here. To begin practicing phenomenological methodology, the researcher must first use epoché, or bracketing, setting aside preconceptions and assumptions that may impede the researcher's openness to learning the meaning of a phenomenon (Plano Clark & Creswell, 2015; van Manen, 2023). Then, the researcher uses reduction, being present and mindful, "turning to" (van Manen, 2023, p. 360; van Manen & van Manen, 2021, p. 1071) the inquiry to be able to be receive meanings given through inquiry and reflect on the essence of the phenomenon. In van Manen's (2023) view of practical phenomenology, the researcher should seek to reduce, rather than deduce or induce, the meanings of the experience through phenomenological methodology (van Manen, 2023). Inductive reasoning is grounded in and derives meanings and themes from the data. Deduction is viewing the data through the lens of an existing theoretical framework (Braun & Clarke, 2024).

van Manen (2023) described reduction as working together with epoché and being a view of the phenomenon without the addition of any conceptions or assumptions. For this dissertation study, the researcher was both inductive, searching for meaning and themes from the data, and deductive, approaching the study through the lens of Critical Race Theory.

van Manen (2023) recommended the researcher consider a partnership of heuristic epoché-reduction and hermeneutic epoché-reduction. With the former, the researcher maintains a sense of "wonder" (van Manen, 2023, p. 368) throughout the inquiry process and lets meaning in ordinary things present themselves. Hermeneutic epoché-reduction requires the researcher to maintain a "radical self-awareness" (van Manen, 2023, p. 369) and reflect on and "overcome[s] one's subjective or private feelings" (van Manen, 2023, p. 369). Methodological epoché-reduction allows the researcher to bracket conventional methodological approaches to the study and improvise with the approach to suit the phenomenon. With neither the time nor the freedom for a great deal of improvisation, this research followed van Manen's recommended compromise: approaching phenomenological research with "heuristic attentiveness, creative insight, interpretive sensibility, linguistic sensitivity, and scholarly preparedness and tact" (van Manen, 2023, p. 372).

Vagle et al. (2024) would have concurred with van Manen that there is no prescribed way to conduct a phenomenological study; the phenomenon itself determines how it should be studied. Vagle et al. (2024) advocated for the researcher's practicing their best judgment as to which processes, techniques, or tools can best "illuminate the phenomenon" (Vagle et al., 2024, p. 226). They suggested that qualitative researchers stay open to emergent research designs and to changing their own design during their study. However, they acknowledged the structure required for research studies like this dissertation study that must go through an institutional review board (IRB), and which require a more planned out structure (Vagle et al., 2024). They recommended extensive study of the phenomenon prior to gathering data "to get a good sense of how it might manifest in the contexts" in which it being explored (Vagle et al., 2024, p. 227). The extensive data gathered for this dissertation research on nursing educators' meanings of the phenomenon of racism was documented in Chapter II of this study. Study site and sample selection are discussed here in the next section of Chapter III. Procedures to be used for data analysis and the role of the researcher are discussed later in this chapter.

Site and Sample Selection

Participants were recruited from among individuals that are known to currently work as nursing educators at Predominately White Institutions (PWIs), and through associates in the nursing profession by way of the snowballing method by email or word of mouth. As this research study centered on Black students at PWIs, nursing educators responding to the survey who were employed at HBCUs, PBIs, and other minority-serving institutions were excluded from the study.

Initially, a single site was chosen for this study. The demographics of the originally planned site are described below. Because of the dissertation committee's concerns about the site's size and the potential that the researcher would not gather enough data to complete the dissertation, plans changed to open the study to a broader group of participants. Two purposeful sampling strategies were employed to select participants for this study: homogenous sampling and snowball sampling. With homogenous sampling, the researcher selected study sites or recruited participants from "a subgroup with defining characteristics" (Plano Clark & Creswell, 2015, p. 334) with the intent of obtaining an in-depth description of or from the group. Snowball sampling allowed the researcher to identify potential sample sites and study participants based on recommendations of other people (Plano Clark & Creswell, 2015). Purposeful sampling allowed the researcher to select a site and group of participants who "can purposefully inform an understanding of the research problem and central phenomenon in the study" (Creswell & Poth, 2018, p. 326). Purposeful sampling was necessary for this study to recruit participants from among individuals who worked as nursing educators (faculty, staff, and administrators) at a PWI at the time the study was conducted.

Some participants worked in dual roles as both administrators and faculty. It is common in higher education that administrators are chosen from among the ranks of tenured faculty (DeZure et al., 2014). Participants with dual roles were asked to choose one role with which they identified for the study. Recruiting of participants was done by email invitation. The sample consisted of educators who worked with students in pre-licensure programs and included educators who reported working for multiple programs in addition to pre-licensure programs. The decision to invite educators of pre-licensure nursing programs was based on personal knowledge, on literature discussing the influence of nursing educators on the professional development and success of nurses in pre-licensure programs (Henderson et al., 2020), and on literature about the coping mechanisms related to racism of students in pre-licensure programs (Attis-Josias, 2023).

The original study site was a four-year public university located in the eastern part of the United States. Eighty-five percent of the students at the university (total undergraduate enrollment = more than 15,000 students) were undergraduates. The study site institution fit the description of a PWI (Clayton et al., 2023; Nguyen et al., 2023). Areas of opportunity identified in the institution's recent self-study included addressing racism, closing racial equity gaps, and better serving underrepresented minority students. Table 3.1 shows demographic data related to

gender, ethnicity, and graduation rates for the originally planned study site.

Table 3.1

Student Demographics for Original Study Site

Key categories	%	2021 Graduation Rates by Race & Gender, %
Gender:		
Female	60	
Male	40	
Race/Ethnicity for total student body:		
White	73	-
Men	-	72
Women	-	80
Black	12	-
Men	-	46
Women	-	62
Hispanic	6	-
Men	-	52
Women	-	64
Two or more races	3	-
Men	-	61
Women	-	57
Asian	3	-
Men	-	73
Women	-	83
Native American/Alaska native	<1	-
Non-resident	-	100
Completion time:		
4 years	55	-
6 years	77	-

Note. The original study site was a public degree-granting institution, primarily baccalaureate

and above, with a Carnegie classification of a doctoral university. The total number of students

at the site was approximately 17,600. Undergraduates accounted for about 82% of the student

body. Ninety percent of students attended full-time, and 40% of students lived on campus. Data

was compiled and adapted from American Council on Education (2023); Institute of Education

Services: Integrated Postsecondary Education Data System (IPEDS): National Center for

Education Statistics (NCES) (2023); Data USA (2023); and U.S. News & World Report (2023).

Data was reported in this dissertation study in ranges or broad terms to ensure confidentiality of the site and participants. The wide range of demographics within the limited number of public institutions with nursing programs in the eastern half of the country influenced the researcher's decision to use ranges or rounded numbers for reporting. The original study site employed almost 2,000 people. Approximately 50% of employees were full-time or part-time faculty. More than 70% of faculty worked full-time. Almost 90% of faculty were tenured or on tenure-track. The faculty was divided almost equally by gender, with there being slightly more females (54%) than males. Most of the faculty (85%) was White. Non-teaching staff comprised the other half of the staff. Among this group were employees that worked in management, construction and maintenance, library science, student services, and office and administrative occupations. The gatekeeper for the original study site gave the researcher written permission to recruit at that site and assured the researcher that Institutional Review Board (IRB) approval was not necessary from that site for this study. Contacting institutional leaders directly and using the snowball sampling method to recruit participants from multiple institutions circumvented potential problems with obtaining permission.

Data Collection Procedures

This section explains choices and procedures for data collection and triangulation. To learn from participants how they understand the problem being studied (meanings of the phenomenon of racism), data was collected through online qualitative written surveys and semi-structured and conversational interviews conducted between individuals and the researcher. Collecting data from three types of sources (faculty, staff, and administrators) and using multiple qualitative methods of data collection assured data and methodology triangulation in this study. Surveys and one-on-one interviews created a safe, non-judgmental space for the participants to explore and share thoughts and feelings on racism that they might not have been comfortable

sharing in the group setting of a focus group (Tilki et al., 2007).

The researcher acknowledged that planning for possible issues was essential to successful

completion of this study (Creswell & Poth, 2018) and incorporated a discussion of planning

throughout this chapter. Data collection was expected to occur during the winter season.

Inclement weather conditions were possible. Weather considerations aside, nursing educators

may work extended hours, have long commutes, and have little discretionary time to engage with

this researcher (Sessler Branden & Sharts-Hopko, 2017). The option to participate remotely may

have been an incentive for participation (Braun et al., 2021). The researcher intended to conduct

all interviews remotely. Zoom, "a communications platform that allows users to connect with

video, audio, phone, and chat" (Zoom, 2024, para. 1), was used for one-on-one interviews. The

Zoom platform allowed for a face-to-face interaction between the participant and the researcher

by way of videoconferencing. The researcher created questionnaires for surveys and to guide

interviews. A discussion of specific data collection methods follows.

Questionnaires and Responses

Questions on the surveys and the interviews were written with slight variations. Interview

questions started with questions that asked faculty, staff, and administrators what they liked best

about working in nursing education. Faculty were asked about their curriculum; Administrators

were asked about how they supported faculty and staff in their roles, and all participants were

asked about working in a culturally diverse environment. Those questions were intended as to

establish a rapport with the researcher, who conducted the interviews, and to warm the

participants up in preparation for subsequent open-ended questions about race, racism, and Black

nursing students. Survey questions varied from interview questions in that they could not be modified, and they did not include "warm up" questions. After asking approximately 15

demographic questions on surveys, the open-ended questions went directly to the discussion of

race and ethnicity, racism, and Black nursing students, so as not to discourage respondents from

completing surveys by asking too many questions.

Online Qualitative Surveys

Online qualitative surveys use questionnaires with open-ended questions. Online

qualitative surveys allow the respondent to type in their own answers, complete the survey

privately on their own schedule, and take as much or as little time as they want to formulate their

responses. Online qualitative survey questions are fixed; questions to prompt, elicit deeper

understanding, or clarify cannot be added during the survey as they can during interviews. Braun

et al. (2021) discuss "breaking the rules of conventional interview question design" (Braun et al.,

2021, p. 648) when creating an online qualitative survey. Open- and close-ended questions may

need to be used together for clarification and to focus responses. An example of this might be

asking a question and then providing a secondary question for clarification. For this study on

nursing educators' meanings of the phenomenon of racism, a closed-end question with a

clarifying secondary question read like this: "Have you witnessed any situations in nursing

education that you would describe as being racist or discriminatory towards another person? If

so, please describe the incident".

Research Questions 1 and 2 (RQ1 & RQ2) were addressed in the online qualitative

survey questionnaire. Online qualitative surveys for this study were administered via the

"experience management" software, Qualtrics (Qualtrics, 2023, para 1). An email invitation

directed potential participants to the questionnaire through a link to Qualtrics survey. The survey opened with the option to give consent to participate, then gave instructions, and moved on to survey questions. A copy of the questionnaire for the online survey is included in Appendix C.

One-on-One Interviews

A typical means of gathering data in a phenomenological study is through interviews (Creswell & Poth, 2018; Vagle et al., 2024). Interviews generate information by eliciting responses through "interactions based on question-answer sequences" (Roulston, 2024, p. 317). Research Questions 1 and 2 (RQ1 & RQ2) were addressed in individual semi-structured interviews. To assist the researcher with keeping organized during data collection, separate interview questionnaires were created for faculty, staff, and administrators. Demographic questions varied slightly among questionnaires. Open-ended questions were similar. Copies of the data collection instrument for interviews are located in Appendices D, E, and F. The data collection instruments consisted of 10-14 demographic questions (depending on the participant's role) and 11 open-ended questions. The researcher added ad hoc prompt questions during interviews to keep the conversation flowing and to elicit thoughtful, meaningful, rich responses. Interviews were conducted at the convenience of the participants and the interviewer without requiring the expensive and inconvenience of travel. Interviews lasted between 15-60 minutes and were conducted on Zoom, "a communications platform that allows users to connect with video, audio, phone, and chat" (Zoom, 2024, para. 1). Meeting on Zoom enabled the interviewer to audio-record the conversation and get transcripts of the conversations. The researcher conducted interviews by Zoom for an unpublished pilot research study in Spring, 2023 and found that interviews were reliably audio-recorded and transcribed by the Zoom application.

Triangulation

Triangulation is a process of verifying the credibility of data by collecting additional information from other sources that will corroborate original findings (Plano Clark & Creswell, 2015). In 1970, Denzin championed triangulation as a means of having qualitative sociological research recognized as scholarly and rigorous when "evaluated against the traditional [quantitative research] "standards of reliability and validity" (Denzin, 1970, p. 98). Denzin (1970) covered triangulation extensively in his seminal work, *The Research Act*. "Because each [research] method reveals different aspects of empirical reality, multiple methods of observations must be employed" (Denzin, 1970, p. 26). Denzin (1970) introduced four types of triangulation: data, investigator, theoretical, and methodological (Denzin, 1970; Fusch et al., 2018). By types of data, Denzin meant person, space, and time (Denzin, 1970). Each source of data represented different relationships to the "events under analysis" (Denzin, 1970, p. 301). Investigator triangulation meant that more than one researcher should explore the phenomenon, with the most seasoned researcher working closest to the data (Denzin, 1970; Fusch et al., 2018), that is observing and coding. Theoretical triangulation involved considering multiple perspectives and theories (Denzin, 1970) such as perspectives of participants in different roles. In this study faculty, staff, and administrators represented three different roles and multiple perspectives. Methodological triangulation involved using multiple methods of collecting data, such as surveys, interviews, and observations (Denzin, 1970). Within or between-method triangulation is a mixture of qualitative and quantitative methods (Denzin, 1970; Fusch et al., 2018). Blended design uses two or more qualitative methods for triangulation (Fusch et al., 2018). Carter et al. (2014) cited data source triangulation – "collection of data from different types of people, including individuals, groups…to gain multiple perspectives and validation of data" (p. 545). Their rationale for this triangulation method (they used two methods in their report: focus groups and in-depth individual interviews) was to gain a broader understanding of a phenomenon. Fusch et al. (2018) discussed the value of triangulation in mitigating researcher bias. The researcher's view will always be present in social research, but triangulation assures that it does not overshadow or replace the view of the participant (Fusch et al., 2018). Collecting qualitative data from three different types of nursing educators, through online qualitative surveys and one-on-one semi-structured interviews, sufficiently triangulated data in this dissertation study via theoretical and methodological triangulation strategies.

Ethical Considerations

The researcher provided potential participants with full disclosure about the study and her position as a doctoral student and nursing faculty. The researcher provided her contact information with instructions and consent forms for interviews and survey (Appendices A and B), offering participants the opportunity to have their questions answered about the study. Participants were provided with contact information for a mental health crisis line if any issues surfaced due to the sensitivity of the phenomenon being studied, and for the university's Institutional Review Board (IRB) if they had further questions. Participants were made aware that they could decline or discontinue participation at any time during the study and that there would be no repercussions for declining or discontinuing the study. Participants were made aware that they would not be compensated for the study. Participants were made aware that the researcher strove to protect their privacy and confidentiality by not recording participants' internet protocol (IP) addresses or names. Pseudonyms were used for interview participants. During the Zoom interviews, participants opted to turn their cameras on. The researcher planned to proceed with audio-only interviews if participants did not consent to video recording or if they become uncomfortable with videorecording during the interview. The researcher bracketed her own personal reflections during the course of the study by journaling and communicating with her dissertation committee chair and consulted with her dissertation chair regarding ethical considerations.

Nursing educators were asked to broadly consider and discuss issues concerning racism and Black/African American students. For the protection of their students, at no time were participants asked to identify, name, or single out specific students. Hardcopies of transcripts were be secured in a locked file cabinet in the researcher's home office. Electronic copies were stored on the researcher's personal hard drive that is password protected. The researcher expected this study to be completed and published by May 2024. The researcher hoped to publish an article in a peer-reviewed scholarly journal subsequent to the completion of this dissertation and will retain data for that purpose.

Approval for the study was obtained from the doctoral candidate's university Institutional Review Board (IRB).

Consent

A link to a detailed, electronic consent form, kept in the researcher's password-protected Qualtrics account, was provided for interview participants. Consents for online qualitative surveys were built into the beginning of the survey. A copy of the detailed consent form used for interviews may be found in Appendix A. Consent for the interview includes consent to record the interview using audio only, audio/video, or no recording.

A copy of the consent for participation in the online qualitative survey may be found in Appendix B. For the online qualitative surveys, the consent request was on the first page of the Qualtrics survey along with the survey introduction (Hanlon, 2022; Redford, 2020). Qualtrics has a "force response" option that required participants to consent to the study before they could proceed with the study questions. Qualtrics also has functionality that allowed the inclusion of

links the participant could follow to email the researcher, get more information on the study, and

seek assistance from outside sources (Redford, 2020). Use of Qualtrics facilitated the ethical

protection of participants in this study. Completion of the consent form and individual's

continued participation in the individual interview constituted the individual's agreement to

participate in the study. A statement to this effect was included in the researcher's introductory

statement for interviews and the online survey. See Appendix C for the online qualitative survey

data collection instrument created by the researcher.

Data Analysis

Data analysis included member-checking of data by providing the participant with the

recording or transcript from their interview (Plano Clark & Creswell, 2015). Data derived

through this phenomenological study was analyzed in a systematic way. In keeping with the

philosophical assumptions of phenomenological research, the researcher prioritized giving

accurate descriptions of what was discovered about the essence of the phenomenon of racism

over attempting to aggregate, summarize, and make assumptions about participants' meanings of

the phenomenon. Braun and Clarke's (2024) reflexive thematic analysis (TA) is a structured

method of data analysis that guided the researcher to uncover themes and patterns in the data and

to structure report-writing for this study. A basic understanding of reflexivity was required to

proceed with the reflexive thematic analysis (TA) approach. Reflexivity is widely used in

qualitative research (Creswell & Poth, 2018; Pillow, 2003; Rankl et al., 2021). Reflexivity is the

critical assessment of self and the intersections of self that the researcher brings to the study

(Lincoln et al., 2024). It is the ability to carry on a constant, iterative, self-reflection during the

study while continuing to hear and reflect upon the participant's meaning of the phenomenon. To be reflexive is to understand one's position, as well as the position of the participant, within the study (Pillow, 2003). To be reflexive is to represent one's position in writing in the report (Creswell & Poth, 2018) This researcher was required to be cognizant of the worldview, experiences, and biases she brought to the research.

> Self-reflexivity acknowledges the researcher's role(s) in the construction of the research problem, the research setting, and research findings, and highlights the importance of researcher becoming consciously aware of these factors and thinking through the implications of these factors for her/his research (Pillow, 2003, p. 179).

Reflexivity is said to have originated in feminist and postcolonial theoretical traditions, both of which emphasized—to help minimize—the divide between researcher and participant (Rankl et al., 2021). Reflexivity as a practice, grew out of the necessity for social science researchers who may have, once upon a time, identified participants as minorities, underprivileged, or in some way lesser than themselves, to acknowledge their positionality and the effect of that position on a study's processes and findings (Pillow, 2003). The expectation of reflexive practice is that the researcher will disclose her position in the study early and with clarity so that the reader is aware of the views and experiences that shape the researcher's approach to the study (Creswell & Poth, 2018). This researcher's positionality is discussed in the next section of this chapter.

One of the hallmarks of the reflexive TA approach is the flexibility of the TA analytic process (Braun & Clarke, 2006). Reflexive TA is guided by research questions, but also guides research questions. Reflexive TA makes it possible for the researcher to refine research questions during the process of data analysis to shift the analytic focus to explore the actual data provided by the participants. Reflexive TA involves six phases: data familiarization, data coding, generating initial themes, developing themes, and writing the report. Phases are not rigidly applied but are guides that support an "organic and evolving" process (Braun & Clarke, 2024, p. 389). The researcher is encouraged to go through the phases thoughtfully and is given the freedom to re-order phases and return to phases as applicable to the research project (Braun & Clarke, 2024).

Reflexive TA calls for returning to the data over and over and deliberating with the data, rather than using software program for data analysis (Braun & Clarke, 2024). So, for this research study, Qualtrics software was used to gather survey data, and interview transcripts were transcribed by Zoom, but the researcher analyzed the data more slowly and manually, as recommended by Braun and Clarke (2024). "Slow" TA did not require extended and excessive time for the project; it did, however, require the researcher to immerse herself in the data, "pondering, wondering, reflecting, imagining, moving away, and coming back again" to the data (Braun & Clarke, 2024, p. 400). If, in the coding phase, the researcher realized that the planned process was not the most effective way to collate the data, she would have solicited assistance from her committee or from a colleague with organizing the data. The amount of time needed to gather sufficient data was unknown during the planning phase of this study. Therefore, the amount of time the researcher could spend with Braun and Clarke's (2024) slow method of analyzing the data was also unknown. The steps that were taken to analyze the data for this study are listed below:

Data familiarization

The researcher reviewed interview and survey responses at the end of the data collection period and selected quotes, themes, narratives that stood out and seemed meaningful in relation to the research questions and interview questions. The researcher spent considerable time with the data during the data familiarization phase: reading and rereading transcripts, listening to audio-recordings, watching videos, going over the data multiple times, thinking about the data, asking questions of the data, and making notes on the data. During this process of interpreting the data, the researcher reflected on the assumptions she made about the data. Data familiarization involved becoming immersed in the data (Braun & Clarke, 2024). The more time she spent with the data, the more this researcher saw individual participants and their responses fade to the background and data move to the forefront. This allowed prepared the researcher to code themes and to report results as aggregate data.

Data Coding

The researcher assigned code labels to meanings found within the data. Code labels should be brief, concise phrases, rather than one-word labels, that "evoke the researcher's analytic take on the data" (Braun & Clarke, 2024, p. 393). Coding can be flexible in reflexive TA. Coding labels were defined and redefined as the researcher developed an interpretation of the data. Coding for this study was both inductive, grounded in the data, and deductive, interpreted through the lens of an existing theory, Critical Race Theory. Coding was both semantic and latent for this study. Semantic coding captured what was explicitly expressed in the data. Latent coding was more interpretive and captured underlying ideas in the data. Meanings understood through immersion in the data were assigned to existing codes or were labeled with a new code. Codes were written in margins or highlighted on hardcopies of transcripts and on a printout of survey data. There were no hard and fast instructions for how to code or when coding is done. However, Braun et al. (2021) cautioned against summarizing and coding responses to each question of a qualitative survey. Their experience was that the most productive data analysis was done across the dataset. When to move from coding to the next phase of generating initial themes was left to the judgment of the researcher (Braun & Clarke, 2024).

Generating Initial Themes

During this phase of the analysis process, the researcher organized ideas captured during data collection into themes or "broader patterns of shared meaning" (Braun & Clark, 2024, p. 395). To generate overarching themes, codes were mapped into clusters, with clusters of concepts then clustered into higher-level clusters or themes. Patterns are made from themes. Important to the reflexive TA process of generating initial themes is the use of iteration. Regarding potential themes, Braun and Clarke (2024) wrote,

> not only are they developed around a central core idea, but they capture multifaceted expressions of that core, with nuance and diversity of meaning from across data items [although any one theme does not need to be evidenced in all or even necessarily most data items] (Braun & Clarke, 2024, p. 395).

Reflective TA aims to develop themes, not topical summaries. Themes in reflexive TA are the equivalent of the elements of the plot of a story. The researcher used her best judgment and consulted with her dissertation committee as to when the story of the data was sufficiently developed to move to the next phase of analysis, developing themes (Braun & Clarke, 2024). The researcher continued the process of reading through and across responses to learn about the phenomenon of racism as understood by nursing educators.

Developing Themes

Developing themes involved reviewing and developing, refining, defining, and naming themes. During this phase, the researcher assessed the themes developed during the previous phase and consider them against the codes generated, against the whole data set, and in relation to the research questions. At this point in the data analysis process, themes were adjusted, or the researcher went back and recoded data. Braun and Clarke (2024) mentioned again in this phase that data analysis is the process of writing the story of the data. Naming and defining themes was the next step in the phase of developing themes. "Struggling to settle on a name that captures the central organizing concept of the theme or write an overall story of the theme in a short (a few hundred words) abstract-like definition, could indicate a theme isn't working" (Braun & Clarke, 2024, p. 397). Naming and defining themes can be done earlier in the process, but the researcher must be willing to abandon themes that do not work, even later in the process. The researcher worked on naming themes throughout the analysis process. With named and defined themes, the final phase of reflexive TA was to write the report.

Writing the Report

Braun and Clarke (2024) included report-writing as part of the analysis of data. They stressed in their description of reflexive TA that data analysis is iterative and reflexive. Reviewing the data, adjusting, and reworking themes with each review, and including the researcher's positionality and theoretical perspective throughout were key activities in employing reflexive TA in this dissertation study. Documenting those activities is an important aspect of reflexive TA. The role of the researcher in reflexive TA is crucial. The researcher was expected to speak for the data and for how she made sense of the data by "[weaving] an analytic narrative" (Braun & Clarke, 2024, p. 398) around the "vivid and compelling" (Braun & Clarke, 2024, p. 398; Braun et al., 2021, p. 650) excerpts extracted from the data in the report. By this time, the researcher had read the data multiple times and had solicited help from more seasoned researchers, her dissertation committee, to check her methodology and process.

Role of the Researcher

The researcher embraced the worldview that research should lead to action and positive change and tried not to take a postpositive approach to this study merely because postpositivism has been "acceptable" in health sciences research (Creswell & Poth, 2018, p. 23). Postpositivism "has the elements of being reductionistic, logical, empirical, cause-and-effect oriented, and deterministic based on a priori theories" (Creswell & Poth, 2018, p. 23). According to Creswell and Poth (2018), many researchers in health science fields—the researcher's profession of nursing among those fields—rely on a postpositive approach to research, relegating qualitative research to a supplement of quantitative research. Postpositivist researchers typically concern themselves with problems, validity, results, reproducibility of results (Creswell & Poth, 2018). The researcher shares the vision of nursing education researcher, Dr. Marilyn Oermann, and of the National League for Nursing (NLN), that nursing *education* research will become a priority for nursing educators. Nursing education research will focus less on clinical matters and more on aspects like faculty practices and innovative educational strategies that can be applied in today's teaching and learning environments (NLN, 2022b; Oermann, 2020).

The researcher may have or have had a professional relationship with some of the potential participants. She was in the role of adjunct instructor and visiting lecturer at a variety of sites from which potential participants may have been recruited. She did not expect her professional relationship with any participants to affect data collection and she practiced epoché or bracketing during the interviews, when creating and refining the qualitative survey, and during the analysis and writing phases of this study.

How This Topic Came to Be & The Researcher's Worldview

The idea for the topic of this dissertation research originated with the researcher's questioning the absence of Black men from nursing education. The research question evolved into a study of the phenomenon of racism from the viewpoint of educators at Predominately White Institutions. Part of the problem discussed in this study is the attrition of Black nursing students. While the researcher did not hypothesize for this study, she certainly has wondered if part of the reason for the attrition of Black nursing students lies with the gatekeepers of the profession. The researcher set this question to the side as she prepared for data collection, analysis, and reporting. Regardless of the outcome of this study, the researcher as a Black nursing educator, positioned herself as wanting to see more Black students, and more students overall, graduate nursing school and resolve the growing nursing shortage.

With a viewpoint that the U.S. has systems and structures built on racism, and that healthcare and nursing are among those systems, this researcher sees this subject through the lens of the first tenet of Critical Race Theory, that racism is normal, common, and an everyday occurrence (Delgado & Stefancic, 2017). This worldview places the researcher in the transformative framework camp. Transformative frameworks require "an action agenda for reform" (Creswell & Poth, 2018, p. 25). Research should contribute a solution to the problem (Creswell & Poth, 2018). It is the researcher's opinion that assisting participants to think about the phenomenon of racism and their hearing or reading their own responses *is* an action.

This researcher is also aligned with the interpretivist or social constructivist camp and would like to first make sense of, or "construct the meaning" (Creswell & Poth, 2018, p. 24) of the participants' experience with the phenomenon of racism. Interpretivism is a good fit for a phenomenological study (Creswell & Poth, 2018). So, the researcher places herself philosophically between social constructivist and transformative frameworks with the assumptions she brings to this research: The participant's reality is subjective and co-created in the mind and through experiences in and with the world, and reality has "historical situatedness" (Lincoln et al., 2024, p. 79). According to Lincoln et al. (2024), "elements of interpretivist/postmodern, critical theory, constructivist, and participative inquire fit comfortably together" (Lincoln et al., 2024, p. 99).

Trustworthiness – Truth Value, Consistency, Confirmability, and Applicability

Validity speaks to the credibility or the truthfulness of an account and its interpretation (Maxwell, 2013). Validation in qualitative research is a controversial topic (Lincoln et al., 2024; Maxwell, 2013). Qualitative researchers choose positions along the spectrum of inquiry paradigms: positivist, postpositivist, critical theorist, constructivist, and participatory (Lincoln et al., 2024, p. 78). According to Maxwell (2013), philosophers [author's note: which would include phenomenologists] position themselves on the other side of the paradigms from positivists, who hold that scientific inquiry must be logical and follow strict guidelines and procedures to be acceptable.

Current literature on qualitative research (Maxwell, 2013; van Manen, 2023) discussed the challenges of applying quantitative language and measures of validation to qualitative research. For this study, however, the researcher is expected to "indicate how accuracy is obtained in representing participants' worldviews" (Cabrini, 2024, p. 33) by addressing four criteria: credibility (truth value/accuracy in representing world views), dependability (consistency/trust in the data and in the research practices), confirmability (reliability), and transferability (applicability/generalizability) (Lincoln & Guba, 1985, as cited in Cabrini, 2024, p. 33; Stahl & King, 2020) as validation strategies. Not all these forms of validation are consistent with phenomenological research, e.g., transferability (van Manen, 2023), and only some forms were used in this dissertation study. For this study, truth value or credibility were checked through triangulation and member checking (Stahl & King, 2020). The researcher's reflexive approach to the research process addressed both dependability (Stahl & King, 2020) and researcher bias as a threat to validity of the report (Maxwell, 2013). Reflexive thematic analysis gave the researcher an active part in data analysis, using researcher subjectivity as a resource, rather than a threat, to the trustworthiness of the data (Braun & Clarke, 2024). For this dissertation study, the researcher sought out an external audit and review of the methodology (Plano Clark & Creswell, 2015) from seasoned researchers.

Creswell and Poth (2018) organized validation strategies by lens - researcher's, participant's, and reader's. They recommended the use of at least two validation strategies. Triangulation may be used to check the accuracy of representations or accounts of a phenomenon through the researcher's lens (Creswell & Poth, 2018). Triangulation is a means of checking truth value or accuracy of world views. Credibility of findings is validated through the participant's lens when the researcher asks the participant to review the data they provide through member checking. Member checking adds richness and trustworthiness of the data by providing participant feedback on aggregate data and on the written data analysis (Creswell & Poth, 2018). This researcher sought assistance from the dissertation committee to check confirmability (reliability). Confirmability meant checking that the research findings were grounded in the participants' responses, and not the researcher's (Stahl & King, 2020).

Validation, consistency, confirmability, generalizability, and applicability are concepts usually associated with quantitative research methods (Maxwell, 2013; van Manen, 2023). van Manen (2023) stated that validity and reliability "apply to tests and measures that are not compatible with phenomenological methodology" (van Manen, 2023, p. 448). "Phenomenological analysis does not involve coding, sorting, calculating, or searching for patterns, synchronicities, frequencies, resemblances, and/or repetitions in data" (van Manen, 2023, p. 35). Rather than attempting to use quantitative methods to generalize, categorize, and fit data obtained into an "empirical generalization" (van Manen, 2023, p. 448), the researcher's focus in a phenomenological study should be on gathering and revealing purposeful information. The researcher aims to gather examples and accounts of lived experiences bounded by person, place, and time (Denzin, 1970). Samples in phenomenological studies do not represent populations, and results cannot be empirically generalizable. It is understood in phenomenological research that outcomes change as studies change, as individual's experiences with phenomena and space and time change (van Manen, 2023). "Phenomenology can give us access to the private and inner lives of particular individuals so that we may know what and how they feel and experience in a particular situation and at a particular moment in time" (van Manen, 2023, p. 371). The experience of an individual is not universal. Nor is it reproduceable, not for the individual in another time and space, and not with other individuals. The ambitious aim of a phenomenological inquiry is to capture and express adequately "what is experienced prior to reflection on the experience" (van Manen, 2023, p. 373). The goal of the phenomenological study is to gather enough examples and make rich descriptions of lived experiences of phenomenon to create a thoughtful and reflective study report.

In review, the researcher attempted to establish credibility and dependability through triangulation, member-checking, reflexivity, and external audit. Triangulation was achieved by employing two methods of data collection and including participants who worked in three different roles. Triangulation adds to the credibility and validity of this study's findings. Member-checking was done by giving interview participants access to their own interview transcripts. Committee members reviewed parts of the data and compared themes with the researcher for external audit. The researcher attempted to remain reflexive throughout the process of the study by bracketing, journaling, and by consulting with her chair.

Chapter IV. Findings

This phenomenological qualitative study sought to explore meanings of racism and the perceived effects of racism on Black nursing students for nursing educators at Predominately White Institutions (PWIs). This study is related to the problem of attrition of Black nursing students at PWIs amidst an on-going nursing shortage. This study was approached through the lens of Critical Race Theory (CRT), with a spirit of inquiry, to gather information and gain understanding of the phenomenon of racism from nursing educators. By exploring meanings and lived experiences with educators at PWIs, this research hopes to examine the prevalence of racism in nursing education and its influence on both educators and students.

The research questions addressed the problems of gaps in nursing education literature related to nursing educators' understanding of racism and the impacts of racism on Black students. Survey and interview questionnaires asked educators to define racism and to list challenges faced by Black nursing students at PWIs. These challenges may be directly related to the problem of attrition of Black nursing students. By asking educators to identify supports in place for Black nursing students at their institutions, the study strove to present evidence that nursing educators at PWIs create—or acknowledge the need to create—inclusive spaces to assuage the impact of racism on their Black nursing students. The research questions that guided this study are

RQ1: What are nursing educators at Predominately White Institutions' (PWIs) meanings of the lived experience of racism? and

RQ2: How do nursing educators at Predominately White Institutions (PWIs) perceive the effects or impact of racism on Black nursing students?

Both research questions are situated within the theoretical framework of Critical Race Theory

(CRT). Two CRT tenets are essential to this study. The first is that racism is an ordinary,

everyday occurrence in the United States (Delgado & Stefancic, 2017). Implicit in this

assumption is the concept of colorblindness that allows individuals not experiencing racism to be

unaware of its existence and effects (Dancis & Coleman, 2022). The second tenet central to this

phenomenological qualitative dissertation study is that narratives are the "cure for silencing"

(Delgado & Stefancic, 2017, p. 50). By telling their own stories about the problem of racism,

nursing educators may become the authors of their own solutions. This research study was

approached with a spirit of inquiry and an understanding that there may be nursing educators at

PWIs who are not knowledgeable about racism or who have not had opportunities to discuss

racism in a safe, non-threatening atmosphere.

Several themes emerged from the anonymous online qualitative surveys and from the

individual interviews. This chapter is organized to present topics and themes gathered from both

methods of data collection. The overarching themes extracted from nursing educators' written

responses on the qualitative survey and from verbal responses from interviews are triangulated

and discussed. Findings are presented as they relate to the research problem and address the

research questions and the CRT framework. Updates to the site and participants, data collection

methods, and data analysis methods explained in Chapter III are included in the next section,

followed by findings.

Updates to Methodology

Broadened Scope for Site and Sample

The plan to recruit participants from a designated site, one for which permission was

obtained from the gatekeeper to contact and recruit participants, was updated to include a broader sample. The primary intentions of broadening the scope were to protect participants and to hear from a diverse group of nursing educators at PWIs. The number of nursing educators at the original site was not large enough to conduct interviews and collect survey data from faculty, staff, and administrators without compromising participants' confidentiality and/or anonymity. Educators at the originally intended site were invited to participate in the study. Additionally, emails were sent to the chairs or deans of approximately 25 nursing programs across the United States. Programs to which emails were sent were selected by the researcher, randomly, from among PWIs and according to whether the dean or chair's email contact was posted on the institution's website. The researcher posted invitations to participate in the study on her professional social media page three times during a three-week period and noted that the posts were seen more than 350 times. The social media invitations included a link to the researcher's email address and a link directly to the Qualtrics survey.

Data Collection Procedures, Survey and Interview Samples

Data collection lasted for four weeks during February and March 2024. By the end of three weeks, 49 individuals had responded to the anonymous online qualitative survey. Surveys were closed at that time as this significant number of responses far exceeded the researcher's aim of at least 15. Ten responses were ineligible, as the close-ended question asking if the respondent worked at a PWI was answered "no."

Thirty-nine individuals self-identified with a "yes" response and met the eligibility requirements for this study. Participants' ages ranged from 32-75 years old (Mean = 50, Median = 49). Additional demographic characteristics of the survey participants are shared in Table 4.1.

Table 4.1

Demographic Characteristics of the Survey Sample

	N	%
Role		
Faculty	28	71.8
Staff	2	5.1
Administrator	9	23.1
Years in Nursing		
0 – 5	7	18
6 – 10	10	25.6
11 – 15	9	23.1
15 – 20	4	10.3
21 – 25	2	5.1
26 – 30	2	5.1
31 – 35	3	7.7
36 +	2	5.1
Years in Current Position		
0 – 5	25	64
6 – 10	7	18
11 – 15	3	7.7
16 – 20	2	5.1
21 – 25	0	0
26 – 30	0	0
31 – 35	1	2.6
36 +	1	2.6
Highest Education		
Bachelor's Degree	2	5.1
Master's Degree	10	25.7
Terminal Degree	25	64.1
Post Doctoral	2	5.1
Gender Identity		
Female	34	87.1

Male	4	10.3
Non-binary	1	2.6
Ethnicity		
White, Non-Hispanic	27	69.3
Black/African American	8	20.5
Latino/Hispanic	1	2.5
Asian	1	2.5
Two or More	2	5.1

N=39

Fourteen nursing educators who identified as currently working in nursing programs at PWIs participated in individual interviews with the researcher. One interview was excluded as it became apparent during the interview that the student population at the participant's institution was mostly Black. The number of interview participants included in this study is 13. The researcher planned to reach data saturation with 12 to 15 interviews (Hennink & Kaiser, 2022). That goal was achieved in this study, with no new themes emerging, after the 9th or 10th interview. Names of interview participants and their roles are listed in Table 4.2.

Table 4.2
Interview Participants and their Roles

Participant	Role
Azalea	Faculty
Daffodil	Faculty
Dahlia	Staff
Daisy	Faculty
Hyacinth	Staff
Iris	Administrator
Jasmine	Staff
Lily	Faculty
Marigold	Faculty
Peony	Administrator
Rose	Staff
Violet	Faculty
Zinnia	Administrator

Interview participants were assigned the names of Spring flowers by the researcher during the data analysis phase. To protect interview participants' confidentiality, participants have not been told their assigned name. Interview participants are referred to in this research report as Azalea, Daffodil, Dahlia, Daisy, Hyacinth, Iris, Jasmine, Lily, Marigold, Peony, Rose, Violet, Zinnia. All interview participants identified as female. Interview participants' roles were faculty (n=6), staff (n=4), and administrator (n=3). Nine interview participants identified their race as White. Four participants identified their race as Black. The distribution of the interview participants by their role is shared in Figure 4.1.

Figure 4.1
Interview Participants by Role

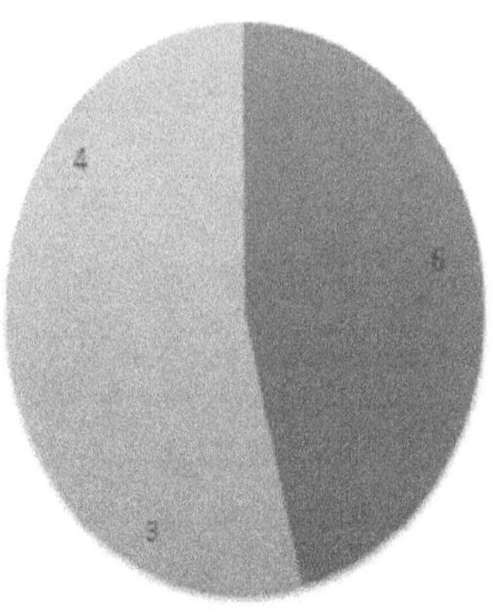

Neither interview nor survey participants were asked to disclose the names of their institutions. Survey participants' locations and institutions were unknown by the researcher. Interview participants represented multiple nursing programs at private and public institutions across two states in the Mid-Atlantic region of the United States. To the best of her ability, the researcher sanitized this report of all information that might identify specific institutions or individuals.

The Process of Data Analysis

Questions asked on surveys and in interviews corresponded to the study's Research Questions 1 and 2. Participants responses were read and analyzed by question and across questions. Findings are reported here in aggregate. Findings were organized into topics. Topics emerged through open and inductive coding. Inductive coding allowed the researcher to discover topics as they emerged. Deductive reasoning was also used. This allowed the researcher to look back and across data for trends. Data collected from interviews and surveys was coded manually and analyzed reflexively, using the steps outlined in Chapter III of this study. The coding strategy was open and inductive—all responses were read through multiple times. The researcher read through and across survey and interview responses to discover initial themes and to develop broader themes.

Coding and Analyzing Surveys

Survey responses were organized into 39 rows, one representing each participant. Questions were displayed as column headers, with responses comprising the contents of the columns. Printing and laying out sheets of data as a large chart allowed the researcher to easily visualize the data and to code manually using colored pencils and making notes in the margins of the chart. Open-ended survey questions were handled individually; the responses to each open-ended survey question were read through multiple times, and initial themes were extracted. Initial themes were then collated into broader themes that represented responses to individual questions. After multiple reads and theme development for each question was completed, the broader themes developed for each question were examined across all the open-ended survey questions for recurrent themes and for ideas that were outstanding but not as common across the data. Uncommon ideas were included in this report as they comprised participants' recall of their own meanings and experiences with the phenomenon of racism and the perceived experiences of Black nursing students.

Coding and Analyzing Interviews

Thirteen interviews were eligible for this study. Two of the 13 interviews were conducted face-to-face. The other 11 interviews were conducted remotely. All the interviews were recorded through the Zoom application, with transcripts provided by Zoom. The Zoom transcripts were clear and legible in many places. The researcher read through transcripts and listened to Zoom recordings in their entirety to fill in missed words and to clarify questionable transcriptions. Participants received a copy of their own transcript for member-checking via an email marked confidential. They were asked to review their transcripts and notify the researcher with omissions, additions, or corrections if they thought any part of the transcript misrepresented the conversation. None of the participants requested updates to their transcripts.

Modifications to Interview Questions

The interview questions that asked, "What experiences with (or exposure to) racism or discrimination against another person have you had?" and "What are your personal experiences with racism in nursing education?" were combined into one question, with the second question eliminated after the 4th or 5th interview. By then, it became apparent that most participants' automatic response was to describe their work experiences. Instead of asking two similar questions, separated by two other questions, a prompt question was included, instead. The question about Black students' engagement was eliminated from interviews halfway through the data collection process as it became clear that participants across roles noted no difference between Black nursing students' engagement and other students.

Findings

Site Demographics: As Described by Participants

Based on responses to the first open-ended survey question, "Please describe the cultural, racial, ethnic diversity of the students, faculty and staff of your nursing program", the nursing programs represented by survey participants were predominantly White. Student populations at the nursing programs represented by survey participants were reported to be made up of 70% to 85% White students. Some responses showed programs with about 5% for each group of students from other races and ethnicities —Asian, Hispanic, and Black students—while other responses showed that there were no Hispanic students or no Asian students in the nursing programs. Race and ethnicity for faculty was reported as slightly more diverse than that of staff and administrators, with 80% to 90% of faculty being White and 95% of staff being White. Some of the qualitative responses were "mostly White", "minimal but improving", "mixed", and "the majority of students, faculty, and staff are White." It seems that at most of the programs represented in the surveys, the student population was somewhat more diverse than nursing faculty, staff, and administration. Participants did not mention the racial and ethnic makeup of administrators at their institutions. Interview participants were asked if they worked "in a pre-licensure, undergraduate nursing program at a Predominately White Institution (PWI)." A PWI was described for respondents as "a college or university where at least half of the enrolled students are White."

Quotations are written in this report as they were stated by the participants, with the addition of punctuation where it was omitted in surveys and transcriptions. The researcher attempted to use the most representative quotations or parts of quotations possible in this report. The researcher also nuanced narratives throughout this report to protect participants, their coworkers, and their institutions, by changing or omitting names of institutions, terminology specific to participants' institutions, and proper names of individuals. Summaries of aggregated data and representative quotations reported here correspond to the research questions of this study.

Meanings of Racism and the Lived Experience of Racism

Findings related to the first research question, *(RQ1): What are nursing educators at Predominately White Institutions' PWIs meanings of the lived experience of racism?* are reported in aggregate and are organized thematically in this section according to the two parts of the question: Meanings of Racism, and the Lived Experience of Racism. Each part of RQ1 was explored with participants via open-ended questions on the survey and interview questionnaires. Responses related to Meanings of Racism, have been reduced to four major themes:

- Racism is Omnipresent and Insidious

- Racism is Painful and Uncomfortable

- Racism Denotes Ignorance and Lack of Knowledge

- Racism is Limiting

Definitions of racism outside of the themes discussed above were provided by participants and are also included in this section of Chapter V. There were three dominant themes related to Meanings of the Lived Experience of Racism. Those themes were

- Fear

- The Angry Black Woman

- Playing the Race Card

The second research question, *(RQ2): How do nursing educators at Predominately White Institutions (PWIs) perceive the effects or impact of racism on Black nursing students?* focused on nursing educators' perceived impacts of racism on Black nursing students. The survey and interview questions posed to address RQ2 asked participants to share what they perceived as challenges Black nursing students face in the participants' nursing programs, and then asked participants to discuss the support systems in place for Black nursing students at their institutions. The five outstanding themes related to challenges faced by Black nursing students were

- Underrepresentation

- Differences or Being a Visible Minority & Being Taught Through a White Lens

- Lack of Preparation

- Friendship

- Class

Study participants were asked to share support systems in place at their institutions for Black nursing students. The survey questionnaire also asked participants to tell how faculty, staff, and administrators addressed racism in nursing education. There were five major themes stemming from addressing racism:

- Individual Efforts

- Avoiding or Ignoring the Topic

- Someone else addresses racism such as Black faculty, the person in the role of DEI administrator, or the dean ("they/them")

- Not doing enough to address racism

- Racism is adequately addressed through professional development, continuing education, and training at the institutional level

A discussion on support systems is divided into survey responses and interview responses. Four interview responses are highlighted in this section. Finally, Chapter IV. Findings, concludes with a discussion on Black nursing educators' responses a discussion about teaching race, ethnicity, and culture. Findings that were unanticipated and not covered in the Chapter II. Review of the Literature were summarized in two topics: Nurses Eat Their Young, and "We are one human race". These topics wrap up Chapter IV.

Meanings of Racism

Participants were asked to define racism. They were invited to use metaphors or imagery and to be creative in their expressions of the meanings of racism. Prominent among definitions of racism were its being present but not always being recognized as being present, being painful or uncomfortable, creating limits and barriers for individuals and for groups, and denoting ignorance or a lack of knowledge.

Racism is Omnipresent and Insidious. An emergent theme in the surveys was that racism is always present but often invisible and not easy to detect. Racism was also described as subtle, yet "evil", "gross", and harmful. Five metaphors shared by survey and interview participants described the omnipresence and subtleties of racism. Racism was likened to an invisible framework, an iceberg, a gnat buzzing around one's head, the smell of a skunk, and a dirty diaper. Imagining racism as the smell of a distant skunk, Interview Participant, Dahlia, said,

> It would smell pretty awful although sometimes it's not easy to detect. Maybe it's a smell that you don't always notice when you're around a lot of other things and then sometimes you'll notice it in different situations more, or it'll be less overpowering it's not always something that hits you right in the face so maybe like a subtle smell of a skunk from far away (Dahlia, Interview).

If it were possible to test the reliability of phenomenological qualitative responses, the survey response written by an administrator comparing racism to a dirty diaper would corroborate the assertations of the present, odorous, yet elusive nature of racism. A faculty participant chose not to use metaphor and instead described the presence of racism in more literal terms, "Racism is gross, is it sad, it is real, it is present today; racism simply is discrimination against another group. Racism can be overt or subtle, it is prevalent" (Faculty, Survey)

The omnipresence of racism was described in surveys as "existing everywhere every day" and "always around." Racism was also defined by survey participants as "a scourge…so insidious that people can easily deny and or justify its existence" (Faculty, Survey). The word, "insidious", was used by three different survey participants (faculty=2, administrator=1). "Subtle" and "unconscious" were also used three times each. "Subtle" was written by two faculty and one administrator. "Unconscious" was used by one faculty and two administrators.

While none of the 13 people interviewed defined racism specifically as being present or ever-present, nine participants responded in the affirmative when asked if they thought about racism in their everyday work. Interview Participant, Jasmine said, "I thought about it a lot, especially when certain comments were made" and described how she had been at the receiving end of what she said were racist comments. Among the four interview participants who seemed unsure that racism was something they frequently thought about, Rose said "it's easier not to think about that when you're surrounded by White people as a White person… it's a privilege that I don't have to think about it all the time." Dahlia stated, "As a very sensitive person that is afraid of hurting anybody's feelings for any reason… I don't really see somebody's appearance in that way." Azalea and Marigold said that they tried not to think about racism. They explained that they only thought about racism at work when they felt they had to speak when colleagues were disparaging or discriminating against a Black student.

I try not to with the students and things like that. But then, when faculty come together, I

feel like sometimes I am. I am their advocate all the time. But when I hear someone

address a student or make an assumption automatically it's like, 'No, don't do that'

(Marigold, Interview).

Racism is Painful and Uncomfortable. Interview Participant, Zinnia, said that racism is "painful to watch." She referred to accounts of racism in the news and racist depictions of Black people in old movies,

It's painful to see that in not so far away in our past it was very prevalent. I think it's

gotten better, but I don't live in the shoes of a person of color, so I don't know it from a

person of color's perspective. I only see it from my perspective which is one of which I

haven't experienced it (Zinnia, Interview).

One survey participant described racism as "a scourge." Another wrote, "The experience of racism sticks in your memory forever with pain." A faculty participant in the survey wrote of their dismay with the current state of racism in education,

There will come a time when it just won't be tolerated to push issues of racism aside. It

pains me that in 2024, we are nowhere near that yet. But I have hope for the future.

Students of all colors are not tolerating the approaches of the past. This will ultimately

drive change for the future.

Another survey response compared the pain of racism to stomach pain. In all, words related to physical pain were used 10 times in the surveys (pain=2, scourge=1, uncomfortable=3, hurt/hurtful=4). Interview participants used the term, "uncomfortable" generously as they defined racism and discussed their lived experiences with the phenomenon of racism. Violet considered comfort in the examples from her clinical practice that she shared in her classroom,

> I tend to teach through stories whenever I can because I think it brings a richness to examples. So, I try hard to bring those examples into the classroom in a way that will be instructive, constructive, and not disparaging and also not make the people in the room more uncomfortable than necessary (Violet, Interview).

Being "uncomfortable" was a feeling interview participants reported experiencing when they thought about racism, witnessed racism, or when they had been accused of being racist. Interviewees Jasmine and Rose reported feeling uncomfortable about sharing on the sensitive topic of racism at work. Rose shared, "It's uncomfortable being in this interview, because I don't want to say something wrong, you know, because I have my own experiences and biases."

Racism is Limiting. Racism was described as limiting opportunities, imposing barriers, or impacting opportunities in the study. The words "barrier" and "limit" or variations of the word limit were used 9 times in surveys. A survey participant wrote, "Racism is what prevents people from being their authentic selves. Racism is the barrier between what some deserve vs what some receive in the workplace" (Faculty, Survey). Racism as limiting was coupled with a conversation that racism affects both individuals and society. An administrator wrote in the survey, "[racism] can limit potential for individuals on both sides of it, when mired in it it can starve innovation, progress, joy and fulfillment both personal and societal." In her interview, Lily compared racism to cancer by describing it as something "that causes dysregulation, that limits the true, the potential of the system. So, if we're operating within the structure of racism, which not *if* we are, we are, we're limiting possibilities in general for everybody." Lily also applied the limitations of racism to nurses' role as advocates,

> Racism can block your ability to advocate for people. I don't want to mash racism and being aware of cultural differences and cultural risk factors and things like that. I think

we need to be aware of those things so that we can advocate. And I think if we're being

racist, we may not be advocating for people in the best way that we can (Lily, Interview).

Racism Denotes Ignorance and Lack of Knowledge. Seven survey participants defined

racism in terms of ignorance or lack of knowledge. One administrator wrote that racism is

"making assumptions based on what you see without knowing a person." Another administrator

wrote on her survey that "Racism to me is ignorance, disrespect, or hatred for a group of

individuals or communities that is different than one's own background."

In comparing racism to an iceberg, a faculty participant surveyed pointed out that for

those people who "don't have to live under the weight of discrimination" is it easy to ignore what

lies beneath the surface. The participant's entire description of racism was,

> Racism is pernicious—For those who don't have to live under the weight of
>
> discrimination, it can be like an iceberg: easy to see the obvious examples above the
>
> surface, but also way too easy to ignore how much is underneath the surface too (Faculty,
>
> Survey).

Interview participant, Daffodil defined racism in this way:

> Racism is essentially treating someone based on their external appearance, not on their
>
> personality or character or what they stand for. It's making a judgment without having all
>
> the information. All you're getting is sight and you're not getting to know what that
>
> person is like or is about or what their life experiences are (Daffodil, Interview).

Other Definitions of Racism. All 52 participants in this study defined racism. Six survey

participants gave responses that read as if out of a textbook or a dictionary, describing racism as

bias, discrimination, or unfair treatment of people or groups of people based on race, ethnicity,

religion, gender, and other characteristics. Rose offered in her interview that she completed a survey and "was trying to use the dictionary definition of racism" in her survey response. Three examples of textbook-types of definitions of racism, written in the survey responses, follow: "Racism is treating someone differently (usually in a negative or discriminatory way) because of the color of their skin" (Faculty, Survey). The words, "negative" or "negatively" were written eight times across survey responses. Another survey participant mentioned discrimination and prejudice in their definition of racism:

> Racism is a belief that race is a determinant of human characteristics and abilities with the assumption that one race is superior to and dominant over others. This results in marginalization of other races, prejudice, discrimination, and animosity towards those who are not perceived as members of the dominant race. This discrimination or prejudice is directed at both individuals and groups, or whole cultures and can result from actions of individuals, groups, institutions or societal systems (Faculty, Survey).

Discrimination based on characteristics was part of another survey participant's response, as well as the concept of systemic racism. Systemic racism was mentioned seven times in survey responses.

> Belief that a person or a member of a group is less than a person or member of another group based on a characteristic. In the case of racism, this characteristic would be race and/or ethnicity. If action is taken based on this belief, it moves to discrimination based upon race. When it is embedded into policies or practices in an organization or society, it becomes systemic racism (Administrator, Survey).

In her interview, Violet defined racism as "designed to put one down and elevate the other another." Daisy was colorful with her description: racism is "a red swath of hate." A descriptive definition of racism from the surveys was, "I think racism is both negatively associating 'prejudice' with the color of someone's skin or their outward appearance/culture, i.e., a person with a head scarf and accent is oppressed; a black dude with a hoodie is a 'gangster'" (Faculty, Survey). Racism as a smell was a creative theme. Iris said, "Racism stinks. If you could think about the most foul odor, whether it was rotten food you forgot about in the refrigerator or you didn't take the trash out, that's what racism reminds me of." If racism had a look, it was "ugly" and "gross" according to two surveys. Racism felt "stressful, violating…lonely" to one faculty survey participant, and "cruel and judgmental" to another. One faculty survey response began with a phrase that was contrary to other definitions of racism shared by participants. However, that response ended with a proclamation against racism: "Racism is a thing in the past, but some people today still have their uneducated opinions/bias. Racism should not be tolerated." One survey participant's response captured the ugly essence of racism, "Racism is the evil troll living under the bridge of life" (Faculty, Survey).

The Lived Experience of Racism

Survey responses. Questions about experiencing a racist incident were posed to encourage study participants to explore the lived experience of racism. Eleven survey participants answered "no" to Question 5.3 which asked if they had ever experienced a racist incident. Five survey participants without experience with racism were administrators. Survey question Q5.4 asked those participants who had experienced a racist incident to describe the experience. There was a plethora of responses to that question. Participants shared their own lived experiences and incidences they had witnessed. Their responses covered several variations that the researcher coded by perpetrator/victim type.

Perpetrator/victim type. Perpetrators and victims of racism were distinguishable in the incidents described by survey participants. Perpetrators were considered by the researcher as those parties which committed or were accused or suspected of committing a racist act. The list of perpetrators included faculty, administrators, staff, students, patients, and the system. The system was defined by participants as "general tendency" or described in terms of processes or systems rather than individuals. Victims were individuals on the receiving end of racist and discriminatory acts. Victims included students, faculty, patients, administrators, and staff. Educators of color were specifically named as victims in at least five incidences. Roles were vague in two responses. Seven incidences described as racist in surveys involved faculty saying or doing something to students; Seven involved the system being racist against the student. Figure 4.2 shows the types of racist incidents reported by survey participants and the number of times each type of incidence appeared in the surveys.

Figure 4.2

Types of Racist Incidents Witnessed by Survey Participants

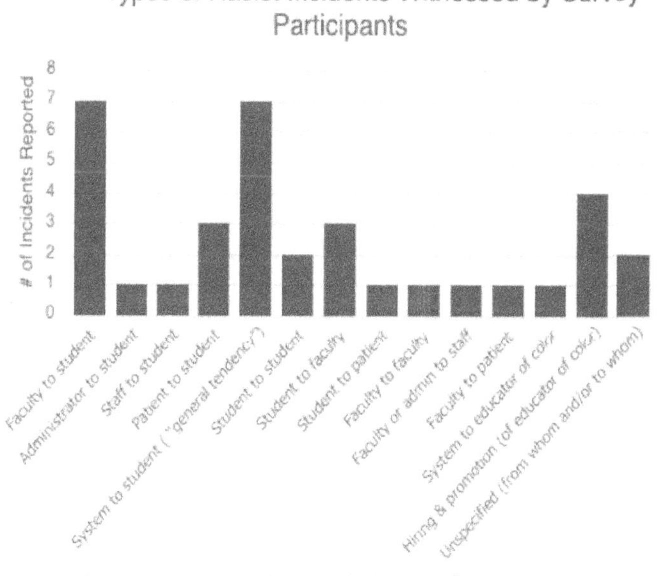

There were six situations from surveys in which nursing students were considered the perpetrators. One participant reported nursing students displaying racist behavior towards patients, "Sometimes see this in the clinical setting from nursing students to patients. Tends to be towards patients with an intersectionality of different identities." Three of the six survey responses involving students as the perpetrator described experiences in which faculty felt they were discriminated against by nursing students. One survey participant who reported her race as White expressed her "hurt" feelings when Black students chose to drop her class and register in the Black faculty's class instead.

> All of the Black students in my class dropped my class so they could join the section being taught by the Black professor (this occurred within the Add/Drop period the first week). This led to a very inequitable situation in which they had 53 students while I only had 46. It struck me that if the tables were turned, faculty would have objected. It did hurt my feelings but what was I to say? Students are free to choose which section to be in, as long as there is space. In the future the cap on the course should be equal between the sections (Administrator, Survey).

In addition to the experience of being White faculty and being discriminated against by Black students, there was the phenomenon of being Black faculty and experiencing the aggression of White students. One survey participant reported,

> I taught one section of a course and a faculty member of color taught another section. At the end of the semester, we were comparing our [student evaluations of teaching] and I was shocked at the way some student comments on her [student evaluations of teaching] included vulgar references and questioned her competency while I did not receive any similar comments. I can assure you that the faculty member was highly competent (I

would say even more so than myself). The student comments also in one instance at least included coded racism (Faculty, Survey).

Another survey participant listed a "bad review for a teacher of color based on her race" among the incidents she experienced. System to student was another type of racism reported in the surveys,

> There is a general tendency at my institution to view Black and Latino students as less bright/talented than white students. They are criticized more harshly and given fewer accommodations. There are not enough support systems to support students of color who may have different needs related to the impact of systemic racism in society (Faculty, Survey).

Interview responses. Twelve interview participants responded affirmatively to having been exposed to racism or discrimination or having experienced racism firsthand. When asked about experiences with or exposure to racism, interview participants framed their lived experiences within a historical context. Hyacinth and Iris described the changes they witnessed as the population of the previously homogenous communities where they grew up or in which they worked changed over time.

> We had a Black family move into our neighborhood and somebody scribbled something on their garage and my father was so upset about it. So, he and some other family members—I was a kid—they went up, knocked on the door, welcomed them to the neighborhood, and asked to help remove the graffiti. So, I know that it's [racism] there (Hyacinth, Interview).

Interview Participant, Iris reflected on racism and the history of the institution in which she was employed and the community where it was situated:

We talk about that area and where people were displaced. It was a largely African American community, largely poor at that point. And people will say it was either urban removal or urban renewal, as the city and the universities that were in that area said that they needed to expand. And you can argue homes weren't kept well at that point. Some homes were. Some people didn't understand property and property values. They were also victims of redlining and other structures (Iris, Interview).

Daisy recalled nursing practice early in her career, "In the seventies we weren't as refined as we are now. Well, definitely, we weren't caring about anybody's diversity." Interview Participant, Peony said she better understood the experience of being different when she took a trip to Africa,

> So, when I stepped off the plane and I was the only White person in a sea of Black people, I totally got it. So, I almost wish everyone could experience being dropped in a place where they're different, and then they understand what people go through every day (Peony, Interview).

Daffodil and Marigold told stories of recent personal experiences with racism. Daffodil shared in her interview,

> The unfortunate part is that I've been somewhat accused of being racist which really goes against my core and what I stand for and what I'm teaching my [child] to stand for. So, it's very, very frustrating…I'm about as White American as you can get. With that said, I do enjoy learning about other cultures and I do enjoy standing for social justice. It's really hard. And I still struggle with how to interpret that and whether there's a lesson for me to learn (Daffodil, Interview).

Marigold recounted being mistaken for a dietary aide while working in the hospital clinical setting with her students,

> I had RN on my badge but the family member was like, 'where's my nurse at?' Like, it says Registered Nurse, you know, and 'I need to speak to the nurse'... and I have my stethoscope and lab jacket. My name's right here with my credentials (Marigold, Interview).

Racism and Fear. Fear was a recurrent expression and is explored in this section. The words "fear" or "afraid" were mentioned seven times in the surveys. A faculty member wrote in the survey, "Racism is FEAR!". Another survey participant used the metaphor of a school bully to describe racism. They explained that the bully targets vulnerable students and gets other students to go along with the bullying. According to this survey response, "if addressed head-on, (the bully) typically runs away fearful."

Fear was a theme in several interview conversations. Out of caution, pseudonyms for interview participants are used sparingly in this section which focuses on educators' fear; race identifiers are used to paraphrase some interviewees and may illustrate different interpretations of the phenomenon of fear. Fear of being considered a racist was a concern voiced by three interview White participants. One White faculty participant described her experience with being accused of being racist by Black students. Those experiences "made me more careful so that I am hopefully not misunderstood... I did not want to be accused of being insensitive." One White faculty interviewed spoke of being unsure if she should call on Black students during class discussions for fear of singling the students out or because she wondered how those students would react. Two interview participants shared narratives about fear and accompanying Black students on clinical experiences. One faculty participant spoke of White adjunct faculty and nursing staff being afraid of Black students,

> We had some junior nursing students, and two of them, one was literally four foot six, four foot seven. The adjunct professor says she was scared of her because the way she talked and this and that. She was scared of the student. The student was Black (Faculty, Interview).

Students' fear and intimidation was addressed by educators, as well. Lily shared how all her students were scared at the beginning of their clinical rotation until they became more confident with their skills. She spoke of a power differential or gradient between instructor and student and how intimidating that could be for students. Azalea discussed White students' fear of going into predominately Black neighborhoods for clinicals. Daisy also mentioned intimidation as a student and going into "edgy" neighborhoods.

Angry Black Woman. "Angry Black woman" (found once in surveys and used by two interview participants), "disrespectful", and "gangster" are labels used by participants in the study that denote what one survey participant defines as "cultural misunderstandings." One survey participant says that they witnessed faculty labeling a student as unprofessional and disrespectful because the student's way of sharing feedback was "rapid fire and verbal and difficult to take in." The faculty doing the labeling preferred "either a slow discussion or written feedback about his performance." According to the survey, the faculty considered the student's way of giving feedback as a challenge to his authority. The angry Black woman trope entered into survey and interview conversations. A survey participant described witnessing a struggling student being labeled an angry black woman. Interview participant, Daffodil shared how saying

"You seem angry" to a Black student resulted in the student becoming offended and ending the conversation.

> The other [faculty] had asked her why, she said, 'you seem very angry, and we're trying to understand where this is coming from'…and the feedback we got later was that she [the student] took offense to that. I don't know that she said it in so many words, but the program director said to us 'you know there's no stereotype about the angry black woman?' No, honestly, I don't (Faculty, Interview).

Lily recalled how she almost mistook a Black student's being "a little standoffish" for a "bad attitude." Lily said she gained insight into what may have caused the student's behavior by getting to know the student better. Lily described the student's "different level of vigilance and suspicion than I would have walking to the dairy farm" as a defense mechanism, not a bad attitude or a sign of disrespect for Lily as faculty.

Participants' responses that mentioned anger, intimidation, and hostility were not all specific to Black women. One survey participant says, "A student was called into the office of a White instructor and told that the police could have been called on her for stalking because the student followed her to the elevator with a question on a quiz." Reflections in surveys such as "continuously proving of oneself" and feeling "the pressure of having an entire racial group of people on your back", and the "expectations that they will 'teach' White students about racism" were among those stated by survey participants, and which could cause a Black student to appear to be angry at times.

Playing the Race Card. Four study participants had discussion around Black students "playing the race card." Interview participant, Rose stated that among challenges Black students might face at PWIs may be that "people like faculty might assume that Black students are 'playing a certain card.'" She recalled hearing people say things like "why do you always have to make it about that?!" when Black students aired grievances or did not get the help they sought from nursing educators

> There will be people who will say, 'Oh you know this person is talking about you're not being equitable towards me" and it was a White person that was saying this and basically shutting down the perspective of a Black student. And I was thinking, 'what do you know about that? You can't just dismiss this out of hand. So, I can see them [Black students] trying to have to fight for things more because maybe certain people like faculty assume they're playing a certain card, and no, that's not what it's always about (Rose, Interview).

During Daisy's interview, the subject arose of students "of a certain population" lobbying for grades that faculty said they did not earn. A faculty member responding to the survey said, "I've heard faculty say 'they'll [the student will] play the race card' if a student is not passed in a course." An administrator wrote about the challenges Black students face at their PWI. The administrator explained that among the challenges faced by many Black students was under-preparation in high school for the nursing math taught at the university level. Of the sessions during which students were allowed to retake the math exam, the administrator's quote is

> Still, I would imagine when students are sitting there looking around and see all the Black and Brown faces in the room, it probably causes a lot of feelings. I don't know what to do about this and have heard many comments over the years where a student who is a person of color is applying layers of racial undertones to situations where it may not be applicable, and it causes great distress for them. Attempts to provide clarity in these situations do not feel appropriate because the students will simply feel as though we are not listening or do not understand. I don't know what to do in these situations either, and

it all feels rather hopeless and defeated. I have had Black students accuse me of being

racist because of recommendations to receive counseling, take a medical leave and/or

drop a course, or the way I do the clinical assignments. When I provide explanations as to

the factors that led to a particular course of action or decision/recommendation and try to

reassure that the decision would be the same for a white student, I am met with the

response that I do not understand what it is to be a Black nursing student at a PWI.

Which, while true, does not change the rationale for the original decision-making

(Administrator, Survey).

Impact of Racism on Black Nursing Students

To explore educators' perceptions of the effects of racism on Black nursing students at

PWIs, participants were asked to identify they challenges they thought Black students faced in

their nursing programs. Survey and interview participants were asked the following question

about Black nursing students at PWIs, "What are some of the challenges you think Black

students might face in your nursing education program?" Additionally, twelve of the thirteen*

interview participants were read a script and asked to expound upon the information in the script.

(*The researcher inadvertently omitted the question when interviewing participant, Peony).

Interview Participants' Thoughts About the Evidence. The script and corresponding

question about evidence of Black nursing students' experiences that was read to interview

participants follows:

Peer-reviewed journal articles that focused on the lived experience of students of color in

nursing school have reported that Black students have described being excluded and

feeling isolated in nursing educational settings. What do you think about this? (the

research findings that were just read)?

Nine interview participants responded that they thought the description read to them about students being excluded or feeling isolated was true or accurate. Iris stated,

> I think that is accurate in some cases. And I think it depends on the students. I found that some of my older, more mature students they can like, 'I'm the only Black one in the group, but I'm going to have my say', whereas some of the maybe younger or less experienced – it's not always about age – won't have their say and will kind of internalize it even though knowing that it's inherently wrong. I was talking with a colleague of mine, this whole idea of handing in an assignment, a group assignment, and if it looked like a Black student had more work on it, then it would get all these markings. But if the White student handed it in, it's like the perfect paper (Iris, Interview).

One participant, Hyacinth stated that she hoped this was experience was not true. Hyacinth said

> I think if it's true, that's awful and I don't see it. We have a diverse group of students, I think and when they come into the office, that's the only time I really see them. So, I don't know if they're being excluded unless I would hear of an issue that came up. Students will come into the office. Sometimes it's two White people, or sometimes it a Black and a White person. Sometimes it's a Hispanic person. I don't notice that anyone is being excluded. And I'm hoping that that's not the case, but it sounds like it is. And I'm not sure how we address that other than if you see it happening, talk to the students (Hyacinth, Interview).

Two interview participants stated that they were not surprised with the statement. Daffodil stated,

> those findings don't surprise me at all especially when you think of the percentage of Black students versus, and I hate to make this about Black versus White because that's not it. What I love is that we have students of all different cultures: Asian cultures,

African cultures, European cultures. You name it. And I appreciate that. But I can see

how, if you're just basing it on race, then I can see how (Daffodil, Interview).

In contrast to the responses affirming belief in the statement, there were two participants whose

responses expressed emotion. Dahlia's statement was, "I'll feel very sad if anybody felt that their

experience was one of isolation and not one of community or acceptance as part of their

educational experience. So, it's very upsetting to hear that." Jasmine said, "That's a shame that

they're feeling that way."

Perceived Challenges Faced by Black Nursing Students. Findings from surveys and

interviews addressing the various challenges faced by Black nursing students at PWIs were

coded into five themes discussed in detail in this section. Those themes are Underrepresentation,

Being a Visible Minority & Being Taught Through a White Lens, Lack of Preparation,

Friendship, and Class. One survey response differed from the others which offered perceptions of

challenges: one faculty participant stated, "I could stand to learn a lot more about this."

Underrepresentation. Fourteen survey participants shared their perceptions of the lived

experience of being underrepresented at a predominately White institution. Five were faculty

participants who listed being underrepresented as challenges. One faculty member wrote in their

survey, "Within the nursing department, there are generally less black students than white or

other races. So, a challenge might be that black student may feel underrepresented and

unsupported" (Faculty, Survey). Another faculty wrote on their survey, "Feeling out of place and

unseen because there are few of them" (Faculty, Survey). Another faculty member wrote, "lack

of role models and other students to share similar experiences with" as a challenge for Black

students at a PWI nursing program.

Feeling the need to prove oneself and "represent" was listed as a challenge for Black students at a PWI. Three faculty participants stated in their survey responses that a challenge for Black nursing students was the stress of needing the represent or prove themselves. One faculty member who completed the survey wrote, "Very limited representation, continuously proving of oneself" was a challenge for Black nursing students. Another faculty survey participant stated, "At PWIs, it's hard to be the 'only', the 'token'…made to feel like they represent all Black people in their encounters." A third faculty participant wrote, "Culture shock. Isolation. Lack of resources. Coming from a position of always having to prove themselves (never given the benefit of the doubt)." Interview Participant, Rose shared her perceptions of the effects of underrepresentation on the students of color with whom she worked,

> We did have a lot of students of color who served…with me. They were definitely, very engaged, very involved. A lot of them were overextended, because I think they wanted to be part of a lot of different organizations to have representation, and to make sure their voices were heard. There's definitely high stress for them because they're trying to perform academically, they're trying to fit in, they're trying to be represented in various ways (Rose, Interview).

Seven survey participants (administrators=2, faculty=5) perceived that lack of Black faculty and staff for mentorship or the limited number of people whom Black students could seek out for support was limiting. "Lack of mentoring from POC faculty" was a faculty participant's response to survey question Q5.5. Another faculty member wrote, "Lack of black faculty and staff who students feel they can go to for assistance and advice or support" as a challenge. Other statements written by survey participants were "lack of diversity among faculty", and "lack of black faculty and staff".

Being a Visible Minority & Being Taught Through a White Lens. There were four survey responses related to the challenges of being a Black nursing student at a PWI related to skin color and being visibly different. Two participants shared in the surveys their perceptions of the challenges of being "visible minorities" or "visibly minority individuals" at a PWI:

> Being in an environment in which they are visible minorities. Interacting with people who have not had prior opportunity or wonderful friendships and experiences with people who were not white. Interacting with people whose prejudice is reflected in their interactions. Also, Black students may feel pressured to make friendships and networks only with people who are similar to them (Faculty, Survey).

Another faculty participant wrote:

> They are very visibly minority individuals and are often interacting with peers who went to largely majority white/upper class educational systems K-12, which means that these peers have had very limited exposure to persons of color. In addition, our Black students often (although not always) come from lower socioeconomic status families, which make it more difficult for them to participate in all the activities that their peers do (Faculty, Survey).

Two survey responses included "skin color" in descriptions of the challenges faced by Black students at PWIs:

> I think there are many challenges Black students might face. They may struggle with feeling different from their non-black, mostly white peers and faculty/staff members in terms of things like just skin color, cultural background, and lived experiences. This can impact communication and a feeling of not belonging to the larger [institutional] communities (Staff, Survey).

> Black students may face issues because their skin appears different, and so they have to
>
> deal with others viewing them as being different (Administrator, Survey).

Five survey participants discussed aspects of "White as the norm" or being "taught through the

lens of mostly White professors". One faculty survey participant stated,

> Black students have to face the idea that they don't belong; some deal with racism and
>
> unconscious (and conscious) bias from other students who do not come from diverse
>
> backgrounds. In nursing education programs, Black students are taught through the lens
>
> of mostly White professors who may also have biases towards ethnically diverse students
>
> as well as outdated racial nursing practices (Faculty, Survey).

Another faculty member responded in this way:

> Black students will hear statistics that put "White" as the norm, even implicitly. Whether
>
> it's positive 'Black women have a lower risk of suicide' or negative 'Black men have a
>
> higher risk of heart disease', both statements are based off a White norm and that gets
>
> very discouraging and unpleasant for students (Faculty, Survey).

"Presenting examples that are relevant to people who have not grown up white and middle-class.

Not acknowledging the differences in how culture impact care and health beliefs", "vocabulary

on testing items", and presenting statistics that may be disparaging, "discouraging and unpleasant

for students" were other comments in the surveys around teaching through a White lens.

Lack of Preparation. Nursing educators saw Black nursing students as lacking the

financial, social, or academic preparation for college. According to Iris, Zinnia, Violet, and

Marigold, many of Black nursing students in their programs were "first-gen", or the first in their

family to attend college. Violet said, "first generation students, regardless of color…don't have the same experience of navigating the higher education system." Iris spoke of lack of financial

preparation,

> I know if you're a student who is a first-generation student, you're figuring out how to
> navigate campus classes, maybe financing your education. If your family hasn't prepared
> or you haven't gotten a scholarship that covers everything, so that's a challenge (Iris,
> Interview).

Being academically under-prepared was mentioned along with being financial underprepared for

college. A survey participant shared this observation,

> Science or other academic preparation from high school. Some are first generation
> students—and first-generation students traditionally benefit from additional guidance
> about navigating higher education. A lot of first-generation students come from a lower
> socioeconomic status/are Pell eligible and may be at a disadvantage from also working
> simultaneously to help pay for their education and possibly not be able to pay to go with
> friends to social activities. I also think there could be a lack of role models— at least it is
> possible the student would have to seek out a mentor (Administrator, Survey).

Interview Participant, Peony noted that many students in her nursing program had the privilege

of attending private and specialty schools where they received a strong foundation in science

courses. She recognized that all the students did not have the same opportunities.

> I really try to deal with things from an academic perspective. Their preparation
> oftentimes is not what some of the other students' are. I don't want to jump in and say all
> Black students don't have that prep, but we certainly have a high level of specialized
> schools that our White population tend to migrate to…so I would say, that science

> background and some of that has been a challenge. So, we try to offer some services here to help with that (Peony, Interview).

When considering her students' backgrounds, Azalea said she sees that the "playing field" is not even for all students. A survey participant discussed lack of academic preparation for math and writing required in nursing school:

> The biggest issues I see are along class lines rather than racial, but they can appear to be along racial lines due to the inequity that exists at the intersection between class and race. For example, students that come from under-resourced secondary schools or are first generation tend to have more gaps with writing and numeracy skills. This puts them behind their peers and causes great distress. I once had a student call me and curse me out because 'we are a racist school where all of the students who needed to retake [math] were people of color, and I am the token white person so you can't be accused of racism.' I reassured the student that all students receive the same preparation and resources for [math], and we have no control over who passes vs. who fails on the first attempt. Some students may need more time practicing or tutoring before being successful, but we do all we can to help ALL students be successful in the end (even if they need all 3 attempts to pass) (Administrator, Survey).

Another administrator completing the survey stated that

> Some Black students lack the academic preparation that many of the white students were privileged to have during high school. This unfortunately has been a challenge as black students need more assistance and support. Our university continually tried to provide added support, but it's not enough (Administrator, Survey)

Not being prepared for the mental and emotional strain of being away from home was a challenge mentioned by faculty participant Marigold. Marigold discussed students need for support to build critical thinking skills requisite to become a nurse,

Sometimes the school that they went to and things like that might be different. So in regards to building upon their critical thinking skills, sometimes they have social barriers, financial barriers…with students of color, I think it's a lot of components that affect their advancement into nursing programs. And the attrition rate is crazy when you think about students of color in nursing programs, it ranges from fifteen to 85% and that is a large range…But why? Is it their critical thinking? Do they have the support that they need? The resources? When we think about equity and equality and all of that, are we meeting their needs? Did I fail the student or did they fail themselves? So, I always think about the resources available. And, yes, you might have a start for the semester your freshman year where it's tough. It's different from high school, but let's get you the resources to build upon your critical thinking so you can be successful (Marigold, Interview).

Friendship. When considering the challenges Black students might face in their nursing educational programs, four survey participants (two faculty, two administrators) discussed difficulty making "friends" or "friendships" as perceived barriers for Black nursing students at PWIs. Being expected to form friendships with other Black students because they are Black was a challenge mentioned by Interview Participant, Marigold, "…maybe they don't get along with that person. You can't automatically assume that they're going to be friends." An administrator wrote in the survey,

Black students may face issues because their skin appears different, and so they have to deal with others viewing them as being different…They may have experienced racism in the past, which may impact their interactions as they move forward in college experience (Administrator, Survey).

Perceptions expressed by a faculty member who participated in the survey are related to the pressure of making friends at a PWI

Being in an environment in which they are visible minorities. Interacting with people who have not had prior opportunity or wonderful friendships and experiences with people who were not white. Interacting with people whose prejudice is reflected in their interactions. Also, Black students may feel pressured to make friendships and networks only with people who are similar to them (Faculty, Survey).

Interview Participant, Jasmine expressed her thoughts on the topic of friendship in this way:

Everyone has the same opportunities…[Black] students have to learn how to break out of that shell, want to be more front and center, if they feel comfortable. I feel as though if [students] keep hiding, [students] will never get those same opportunities (Jasmine, Interview).

A survey participant echoed Jasmine's opinions with a similar response,

I would say the biggest challenge facing Black students in our program is the intersection of class and race and what it means to be a minority person spending a significant amount of time with the majority group, and how that shapes one's perceptions of various situations and interactions. Also, their opportunities to bond/connect with their fellow students may feel limited and require them to be more assertive and "put themselves out there" whereas other students may have an easier time finding/making friends. Very challenging indeed (Administrator, Survey).

Survey and interview participants discussed students' lack of financial resources and need to work to pay tuition as other possible barriers for Black students to attending social activities and forging friendships. One survey participant wrote about how Black students often make friends with other Black students out of necessity,

> Feeling isolated. There aren't that many Black students and I know that some students feel that there are so few that they end up with the other students ONLY because they are Black, even if they don't actually have that much in common (Faculty, Survey).

Class. Socioeconomic class was mentioned in six survey responses. The term, "class" was used three times in response to survey question Q5.5, which asked educators about the challenges they thought faced Black nursing students faced in their programs. In addition to posing a challenge to Black students at PWIs, class was also used by one survey participant to define racism, used by another survey participant to describe the cultural, racial, and ethnic makeup of their institution, and mentioned in one experience with racism shared by a survey participant. Classism was described by a faculty survey participant as being as big a challenge for nursing students as racism,

> I would say the biggest challenge facing Black students in our program is the intersection of class and race and what it means to be a minority person spending a significant amount of time with the majority group, and how that shapes one's perceptions of various situations and interactions (Administrator, Survey).

A faculty member responding to the survey question about challenges wrote that families' socioeconomic class and the class of schools attended were factors affecting students,

> They are very visibly minority individuals and are often interacting with peers who went to largely majority white/upper class educational systems K-12, which means that these

peers have had very limited exposure to persons of color. In addition, our Black students often (although not always) come from lower socioeconomic status families, which make it more difficult for them to participate in all the activities that their peers do (Faculty, Survey).

Class was mentioned in response to the open-ended demographic question asking survey participants about the cultural, racial, and ethnic makeup of their nursing program. One faculty participant noted that most of their faculty and students hailed from predominately White, middle-class backgrounds:

The faculty are largely, though not entirely, homogeneous in their cultural, racial, and ethnic background. Mostly White, mostly from upper middle-class backgrounds. Even for those people who are of different cultures, they have to learn to operate within that cultural 'space'. The students have some more diversity, but it's still predominantly White, predominantly upper middle class. Students that fall outside of this have told me that they often feel out of place or that teachers talk about their own cultural backgrounds as 'interesting examples' rather than people (Faculty, Survey).

Other Challenges. Study participants shared perceptions of effects of racism on Black students and the challenges Black students faced that were not included among the themes discussed earlier in this section. "Feeling 'othered'. Microaggression. Expectations they will 'teach' white students about racism" were some of the perceived challenges for Black students that were noted by a faculty participant in the survey. A staff survey participant proffered another perspective of the challenges at PWIs: "Cultural misunderstandings. Some people were raised differently, and their standards are different. Doesn't mean they are weird or strange, just that their value systems are different from others" (Staff, Survey). Marigold shared in her interview that she felt that pride was a barrier preventing many nursing students of color from seeking the support that they need,

> Another challenge is their pride. They don't want to admit that they need help because their family has these expectations and sometimes it's the pressure of being that nurse. So, I think it's their pride where they don't want to say that they need help or they may feel less than if they seek out tutoring, mental health, and things like that. So, another challenge is mental health. We know that there's an increased number of cases of depression and anxiety with college students (Marigold, Interview).

Addressing Racism in Nursing Education

After they identified challenges in written survey responses and in interviews, study participants were then asked to tell how nursing educators addressed racism. Survey question Q5.7 asked, "How do faculty, staff, and administrators address racism in nursing education?" The wording of the survey question allowed for responses to be written in the past, present, or future tense. There were three different types of responses to this question: survey participants wrote about themselves, their colleagues and other individuals, or they wrote about programs and systems at their institutions. Five sub-themes that emerged from the three types of survey responses to the question of addressing racism in nursing were

- individual efforts
- avoiding or ignoring the topic of racism
- not doing enough to address racism
- someone else such as Black faculty, the person in the role of DEI administrator, or the dean, addresses racism

- racism being adequately addressed through professional development, continuing education, and training at the institutional level

Individual efforts. Three short survey responses mentioned individual efforts to address racism through examination of one's own biases. One survey response written by a faculty participant was, "Begin with evaluating their own inherent biases." An administrator stated in the survey, "Becoming aware of bias." Another faculty participant wrote, "Personally I work to acknowledge my own implicit bias and seek to learn about the experience of others."

Avoiding or Ignoring the Topic. "Avoidance" was mentioned by three nursing faculty as a strategy for address racism. One of those survey participants wrote,

I think that many people avoid the topic all together out of fear of "offending" someone. I do incorporate teaching on health disparities, microaggressions and inclusivity into my courses and also try to be sure to showcase a diversity of skin tones, races/ethnicities in my PowerPoint images and class case studies. I also try to be sure to avoid only discussing race when it revolves around negative outcomes (i.e. I try to highlight positive resilience and outcomes as well as health disparities and I avoid using individuals of color in case studies focused on poor self-care/non-adherence/addiction, etc.) (Faculty, Survey).

Someone Else Addresses Racism. Eleven survey participants addressed nursing educators other than themselves as "they or them" and as answerable for addressing racism in nursing education. This analysis was made by reviewing responses that included the terms "they" or "them", did not include the terms "I" or "we", and did not any wording that explicitly stated that the participant took an active role in addressing racism. Responses that did not name specific strategies, roles, offices, or systems in place to address racism, regardless of the participant's stated participation, were also counted. Others study participants questioned nursing educators' ability or willingness to address racism. One faculty participant wrote, "They might give lip service to being equitable, but few of them are truly anti-racist." Another faculty member wrote in the survey, "I don't think they do, and it pisses me off! If I were an administrator, I would be holding everyone accountable."

In survey responses to question Q5.7, which asked how nursing faculty, staff, and administrators address racism, DEI (Diversity, Equity, and Inclusion) departments, deans and other administrators, and Black faculty were frequently named. "We have a DEI department where you can express your concerns." At one institution there was a DEI committee which "lost momentum" after the director resigned. At another institution, "they asked the one or few Black faculty to come up with solutions to racism." Another participant noted that Black educators facilitated events which often take place during "non-business or school hours."

Not Doing Enough. A faculty participant wrote of their nursing program's addressing of racism, "content is threaded throughout curricula, but we can always do more." Another faculty survey participant stated that some educators are proficient at addressing racism by acknowledging racism as a problem and incorporating that acknowledgement in their teaching, "rather than in unique 'racism' units or classes."

Adequately Addressed. Six participants responded that continuing education and professional development were ways that nursing educators addressed racism at their institutions. "We have mandatory videos we watch." There were two responses that stood apart from others: One faculty wrote on their survey, "I have not experienced any occasions in which we needed to address racism." A staff participant wrote, "Sometimes students will try to stack the deck in their favor to get the outcome they desire." Seven participants wrote that nursing educators addressed racism in nursing by taking personal accountability to evaluate their own biases. One of those participants thought it productive "to self-monitor attitudes and behavior to avoid racism." Another participant said they "incorporate teaching on health disparities, microaggressions, and inclusivity into [their] courses and also try to be sure to showcase a diversity of skin tones, races/ethnicities."

Support Systems for Black Nursing Students at PWIs

Survey Responses. The survey questionnaire asked participants to "Please share the support systems in place for Black students in your nursing program." Responses varied. Two participants left this response unanswered, one staff and one faculty. Support systems listed in surveys ranged from nothing in place to reports of several entities in individual nursing programs that supported Black nursing students. One faculty participant responded, "I don't know". The one staff participant who responded to question Q5.6 wrote, "It seems that the Black faculty, staff, and administrators shoulder most of the burden to advocate for and support Black students" (Staff, Survey). The three survey participants who reported that there were no supports in place for Black nursing students at their institutions were faculty. One faculty reported, "None. There was a DEI person, but she left year and half ago. I don't know who is in place now myself so I'm sure they don't know" (Faculty, Survey). The outlying response to Q5.6 stated, "systemic racism" in answer to this question. The participant responding identified as faculty and responded to the next question (Q5.7) about addressing racism, "They ask the one or few Black faculty to come up with solutions to racism" (Faculty, Survey). Three participants, all faculty, identified institutional-level resources, outside of their nursing programs, as they only supports for Black nursing students. Those responses follow: "None in the nursing program, but some present at university level"; "Black student groups on campus"; and "Minority group support in place on a university level."

Thirty of the 39 survey participants responded to question Q5.6 listing support systems in place at their nursing programs with responses other than "none", "I don't know" and blanks. The term, "multicultural" was used 14 times in the survey to describe student nursing groups present as supports for Black students. The term, "inclusive excellence" was found eight times across survey responses, listed once as part of a strategic plan and seven times within the phrase, "dean of inclusive excellence." The word, "minority" was used four times in descriptions of support systems for Black nursing students: once by a survey participant to describe herself, "My students have me they know I am a minority and they sometimes talk to me about that" (Faculty, Survey), once to describe students, and twice to label student groups on campus. The word, "black" was used 20 times in Q5.6 of the survey. Survey responses that included the word "black" when naming support systems for Black students included four references to Black advisors or faculty mentors; one center for Black students; one university-level Black men's group; five responses with non-specific or unnamed entities on campus that supported Black students; three Black student-organized groups on campus, including two social media groups; two references to sororities with mostly Black membership; two references to a state-level Black Nurses Association.

Quotations representative of the 30 survey participant responses to the question about support systems for Black nurses follow:

Students in the nursing department have access to all the university programs developed

to help ensure minority students have resources, tutoring, and counseling to be successful and complete their degrees. Every student has an advisor, and every faculty member can make a referral for struggling students (Faculty, Survey).

"There are different cultural groups, in school and at University resources, and faculty who are viewed as safe spaces." (Faculty, Survey)

Associate Dean at who focuses on diversity and inclusion and a university-wide initiative for inclusiveness. A multicultural nursing student organization. A required course focusing on racism, through the Student Nurses Association, scholarships sponsored by Johnson & Johnson in their 'Race to Equity' initiative supporting nursing students of color. A new program at [nursing program] with alumni mentors of color. The Student Nurses Association is one of the most diverse groups on campus as it unites nursing students from all programs and backgrounds at [nursing program]. The academic advisor system also provides support. In addition to support systems mentioned, support also comes from people (Faculty, staff, peers) who are not Black. Although there is a long way to go, sincere initiatives have begun (Faculty, Survey).

"Extensive. We have three support counselors and an Assistant Dean of Student Success" (Administrator, Survey).

The support systems are as follows: Student nursing group for people from multicultural backgrounds, a center for black students, tutoring and support from a black advisor, a movement on campus for DEI— which has provided specific support and safe space for these students to study and come for questions (Administrator, Survey).

"multicultural student group, black faculty mentors, black sororities" (Faculty, Survey)

There are support systems for all students but not specifically black students. This actually sparked an idea to introduce students to other nursing organizations such as the Black Nurses Association or others like Hispanic Nurses Association. I know in another state where I practice, these organizations are more prevalent but I have not seen any advertisement for these organizations at my University (Faculty, Survey).

"The office of student success is a bridge to academic support services including academic coaching, tutoring, mentorship, academic advising, career advising" (Administrator, Survey).

The college has an educational specialist who supports all students, not just students of color. The university has an office to support students but is not expressly dedicated to students of color and is chronically understaffed/underfunded. The college does have a Dean for DEIA and the university does have an Office of DEIA. The college has several student organizations for students of color. The faculty is not as diverse as it could be which limits the number of role models for students who are like them and is a source of stress for faculty who do serve as role models. In general, there is more talk of support than actual support provided (Faculty, Survey).

"Office of Intercultural Affairs does a ton of programing. DEI Office hosts affinity groups" (Faculty, Survey).

We have a dean of inclusive excellence in the nursing college who is strategic in improving the experience of racial and ethnically diverse students. There is also a [name] organization that brings together students with textured hair. There is also a multicultural student nursing org that was created by students of color who wanted an experience of belonging. It is an org to bring together multicultural students and share like experiences. I do not know of any other supports for Black students in my program (Faculty, Survey).

"It seems that the Black faculty, staff, and administrators shoulder most of the burden to advocate for and support Black students." (Staff, Survey).

Interview Responses. Interview participants shared details about their activities and their reasons for being directly involvement as supportive systems for Black students. Violet shared her volunteer experience working with Black students in a national mentoring program, Rose talked about supporting Black student-led events, Zinnia said that she supported Black faculty events and was able to help her students find finances to pay for school, and Peony shared how she assessed students' needs to see if she could help them instead of immediately sending them to talk with someone else.

Violet. Violet opened her interview with a narrative about how being a first-generation student herself prompted her to volunteer through a national program to mentor other first-generation students.

> It's a foundation where you take individuals from a specific city or geographic area and you enroll them in higher education, or they get accepted to a higher education program as a cohort. So, they have their posse. They have their support system…I think about the things I didn't get or that I didn't know that people didn't know. The people around me didn't necessarily know how to help me (Violet, Interview).

Peony. In her interview, Peony offered communication as the key to understanding the needs of students of color, and of all students. Peony stated that her practice is to listen to students to learn how she can help them.

> I hate to just label them and send them to all these systems, though sometimes it is just a discussion. So, I'll bring them in and I'll talk to them. And just what do you really need? Because I don't want to just assume that they need another space to go and talk to

somebody that looks like them. I think sometimes it's not always about that, and that

sometimes they're tired of that (Peony, Interview).

Rose. Rose shared her support for a Black student group at her institution by attending an

event they sponsored.

I was at a mental health event sponsored by the Black Alumni Association, and kind of

naively thought that a lot of other White people would go because, oh, they're sponsoring

it, just as if it were sponsored by anybody, and just about mental health. And I went, and I

was the only White staff member there that wasn't either hosting or [the university

president] (Rose, Interview).

Zinnia. In her interview, Zinnia told the researcher that she regularly attended an annual

lecture series sponsored by Black nursing faculty. She also talked about the academic, financial,

and emotional support that she was able to provide for her students through her administrative

role.

I'm always learning from my students about their cultural differences. Sometimes things

will come up in advisement sessions. Sometimes they'll come up because the student is

not doing well, and so we talk about what's going on in their life and their background

and so on. And sometimes it's impacted by things that are cultural in nature or family-

oriented in nature in addition to whatever the educational situation is. For example,

maybe they have to work. They have to self-support. So that impacts their ability to

complete the program easily and comfortably. So, any of those kinds of things that come

up, that I need to help support them for or things that I then try to deal with in some other

way, whether it be finding some resource for them academically, emotionally, or financially. Educationally, too. I try to match a resource with whatever the need is

(Zinnia, Interview).

Lived Experiences of Nursing Educators

Nursing educators interviewed for this study were asked, as warm-up questions preceding

the questions on racism and Black students, what they liked best about working in nursing

education. Faculty were asked what they liked about the curriculum in the program(s) in which

they taught. Participants expressed contentment with their work, as evidenced by the following

responses:

> I'm very enthusiastic about teaching and about learning and about really understanding
>
> things rather than just memorizing them…I also am very committed to patient advocacy
>
> in all different types of forms. And that's one of the things I really enjoy, instilling in
>
> students to be advocates for patients. I've grown to appreciate simulation over time, so I
>
> think the simulation part of our curriculum is really important…In simulation, when
>
> they're left to their own devices, that those knowledge gaps or those things become
>
> apparent. And that's when the lightbulb moments happen (Lily, Interview).

Daisy shared:

> The expansion of my knowledge, and also the feedback from the students when they
>
> learn something new. I also like the flexibility in nursing education as a faculty member.
>
> [About the curriculum]: I think it's very care centered, patient care centered and very
>
> centered on social determinants of health across populations (Daisy, Interview).

Black Nursing Educators' Responses. There were four nursing educators interviewed

who identified as Black/African American. Their pseudonyms and roles will not be shared in this

section, to protect their confidentiality. Each Black interview participant had a personal story to share about her own experience with racism in nursing education. Participants spoke of earning their titles and needing to show and prove that they were qualified to be in their positions and capable of doing their work. One narrative that was shared by two participants was that of working with students in the clinical setting and not being acknowledged by patients and clients or other healthcare professionals as the registered nurse in charge. They shared that they have worn their white lab coats in clinical settings where lab coats were not usually worn so that would recognize that they were, in fact, the clinical faculty supervising the nursing students. One participant told the story of having a patient address her as a dietary aid while she was instructing her students. She said she was wearing a stethoscope, her white lab jacket, and a name tag that said she was a registered nurse. Three Black interview participants spoke of disrespect and shared that they had experienced while working in the discipline of nursing education. Among survey participants, Black faculty, and White faculty who said they worked closely with Black faculty, wrote on surveys about Black faculty being "disrespected" by students in the classroom and on student evaluations of teaching. One Black participant in the interviews described how she and a White colleague team-taught the same course and "split the grading…I've had the line outside my door questioning my grading, but not questioning my counterpart." Black faculty described having their knowledge and authority challenged in the classroom and in the clinical setting. A Black educator interviewed for this study called such behavior "disrespect" and resulting from "conditioning." A White survey participant wrote that she and a faculty member of color taught two sections of the same course. When they were comparing their student evaluations of teaching, the White faculty member was shocked that the comments on the faculty of color's student evaluations included "vulgar references and questioned [the faculty of color's] competency." The survey participant wrote that she did not receive similar comments and, "I can assure you that the faculty member was highly competent. (I would say even more so than myself). The student comments also in one instance at least included coded racism."

Black nursing educators shared narratives and experiences that were not shared by White participants. Black faculty's narratives included being expected to be the provider of all support to Black students: academic, emotional, and social. Two interview participants said they had been given a heavier workload than their White counterparts. One educator wrote in a survey how a colleague who previously knew her name and used it frequently began calling her by the name of the new Black educator hired after her. "It's as if I never existed to her as a faculty member. It makes me think it's more natural for her to interact with Black people as subordinates rather than equals."

On Teaching Race, Ethnicity and Culture. Faculty were not specifically asked to discuss if or how they teach about race, ethnicity, and culture. However, when asked how working with people from other races, ethnicities, or cultures influenced their work, four faculty interviewed talked about incorporating culture into their lectures, class discussions, or clinical experiences. According to Marigold, "everyone should incorporate that cultural perspective in your lectures." She said she does that by engaging her students in discussion to get different perspectives. She described having a rapport with her students that allows them to feel safe raising their hands and giving their perspectives on what they're studying that day. Lily said she tries to encourage students to teach her and to teach their peers in the classroom and the clinical settings by sharing their experiences "to whatever extent they are comfortable."

Violet, Lily, and Azalea spoke about how race has traditionally been taught as a determinant of health or risk factor in nursing education. They spoke of how race is a social construct and how they came to be intentional about how they incorporate that discussion into their lectures. These faculty specifically used the words, "race" and "racism" in their conversations about teaching. They recounted experiences from their clinical practice where racism was a factor in patient care. Violet and Lily stated that they have placed more emphasis on how they teach about race over the course of years of seeing their nursing programs become more diverse. Azalea credits life experience as her inspiration. She states that she was taught in a nursing program where there was a lot of support for students of color.

The way nursing educators were taught when they were students came up in interviews. Violet spoke about how once upon a time healthcare providers were taught that, "skin color changes your pain perception" and that certain groups of people could not be treated with the "same type of pain medications because they'll just become addicts." She said she shares this information with her students so they will be aware that there are providers still in practice that adhere to the discriminatory practices that were foundational to their education.

Nurses Eat Their Young. The adage, "nurses eat their young" came up in two interview discussions about nursing faculty teaching the way they were taught. Violet described "nurses eat their young" as an aggression of nurses towards new nurses as a rite of passage or "paying your dues." She described this socialization into the nursing profession in which seasoned nurses taught new nurses the way *they* were taught, "We've always been aggressive towards the new nurses because we had to teach them the way you were taught. And you know this whole paying your dues concept is really very destructive" (Violet, Interview). Part of Violet's socialization into the profession was being told by a registered nurse with a two-year degree that if she [Violet] pursued a Bachelor of Science (BS) in Nursing, she would be a BS (bullshit) nurse.

The older nurse in the practice looked at me and said, 'Oh, you're gonna be one of those

BS nurses.' You know, bullshit nurses, because I was going to get a four-year degree

> instead of a two-year degree, and nursing has done that for decades. We have put down
> students or nurses that were seeking higher education. And then we look at students who
> maybe are of color of maybe don't have the same resources as our other students and say,
> 'Well, why are they here. They belong in a two-year program. They'd be better off in a
> two-year program. They can be a nurse. They just can't be one here'…It doesn't have
> anything to do with your appearance or the melanin in your skin (Violet, Interview).

Iris also used the term, "nurses eat their young" in her interview.

> You know we hear about 'nurses eat their young'…that just really drives me crazy. But I
> make sure that the students are held to a standard because I hold myself to a standard. I'm
> not asking them to do anything that I haven't (Iris, Interview).

"We are one human race". The need to get along together because "we are one human race" was expressed by Dahlia and echoed by Peony and Lily. Peony pointed out in her interview,

> I wish people wouldn't always see the differences in people and see more of the
> similarities in the fact that we're all human. So, I think it's ugly racism because it pushed
> people down that don't deserve to be pushed down and we should all being trying to
> figure out ways to bring people up (Peony, Interview).

Lily stated, "we just need to be humans together." She summarized her interview with how "this is very, very complicated; not black and white." An administrator wrote in the survey, "racism is not just Black vs. White in academia. There are many other forms and occurrences in nursing departments" (Administrator, Survey).

Chapter V. Conclusions, Discussion and Recommendations

This phenomenological qualitative research study was conducted to explore meanings of the phenomenon of racism and the effects of racism on Black nursing students for nursing educators at Predominately White Institutions (PWIs). The research study was designed to address the study's two research questions through online qualitative surveys and individual face-to-face interviews conducted with nursing educators. The research questions for this study were

RQ1: What are nursing educators at Predominately White Institutions' (PWIs) meanings of the lived experience of racism? and

RQ2: How do nursing educators at Predominately White Institutions (PWIs) perceive the effects or impact of racism on Black nursing students?

Nursing educators included in this study were administrators, faculty, and staff currently employed at an undergraduate nursing program at a PWI. To make conclusions and recommendations in Chapter V, research findings were examined alongside literature and evidence previously presented in Chapters I and Chapters II of this study. Findings related to RQ1 showed that racism was defined in various ways. Seven major topics emerged as meanings of racism and the lived experience of racism. There were five themes related to nursing educators' perceptions of the impact of racism on Black nursing students. Findings are addressed relative to their connection to or conflict with the larger body of literature and their alignment with the theoretical framework, Critical Race Theory. Limitations, implications of this study for the field of nursing education, and recommendations for practice and future research are included here. A narrative, written to acknowledge and honor the CRT tenet of storytelling concludes this chapter.

Discussion of the Findings

Generally, most study participants responded to all of the open-ended questions, except for Q5.8 which asked survey participants if they had anything else they wanted to discuss about their knowledge and experience of racism in nursing education. Seventeen of 39 educators responded to that question. There were two blank responses each for the following questions: Q5.4 (two participants who responded, "yes" to Q5.3 did not elaborate on experiencing or witnessing racism in Q5.4), Q5.6 which asked how staff, faculty, and administrators address racism in nursing education, Q5.7 which asked participants to share the support systems in place for Black students at their nursing programs. All survey participants responded to the challenges that Black students might face in their nursing education programs. All survey and interview participants gave definitions of racism.

The overarching ideas expressed through the surveys were that racism exists, racism poses limitations and is a barrier, racism is a form of discrimination against individuals or groups of people based on traits or characteristics such as skin color, and racism is associated with fear. While there were responses in this study that stood out from others, there were no outliers in the statistical or quantitative sense of the word. Each response was considered a lived experience of the participant, unique to that individual and couched within their own telling, time, and space.

Most of the responses to this study's survey and interview questions indicate that there was consciousness and intentionality to be sensitive and to not be racist towards students of color. There was an awareness that students of color face challenges that are above and beyond the challenges that white students face at PWIs. The findings of this dissertation study are consistent with descriptions of the many challenges faced by Black students at PWIs as documented in the literature reviewed in Chapter II of this report (Eudy & Brooks, 2022; Harris et al. 2014; Matthews et al., 2022; White et al., 2020; White & Fulton, 2015).

Thirty out of thirty-nine survey participants of this dissertation study named support systems in place at their institutions. Additionally, nursing educators interviewed mentioned their personal efforts to address the specific needs of Black students, providing direct support for Black nursing students, or being part of a group or organization with a specific purpose of supporting Black nursing students. Findings indicated that supports for Black students and efforts to address racism in nursing education sometimes reside within the same structures. Support systems in place for Black nursing students are often administered by entities such as

- college deans

- multicultural groups

- offices and directors of DEI

- deans of inclusive excellence

- other administrators

- affinity groups outside of nursing

Survey findings indicate that Black nursing educators bear the brunt of the responsibility for creating and maintaining structures that support Black nursing students at PWIs. Faculty and administrators interviewed for this study, both Black and White, shared specific ways they supported or could support Black students. Marigold spoke of creating mentoring programs. Violet shared her volunteer experience working with Black students in a national mentoring program. Azalea told how she spoke up for students when they needed advocacy. Lily shared how she worked to get to know her Black students better and to help all her students work collaboratively in the clinical setting. Peony stated that she talked with students to find out what they needed before sending them to someone else. Iris spoke of being accessible and maintaining an open-door policy on campus and at community sites. Rose attended functions such as lectures sponsored by Black student groups. The caring behaviors displayed by study participants who worked directly to address racism in nursing and to support Black nursing students connect to evidence presented by Henderson et al. (2020) and Matthews et al. (2022) about nursing educators' influence on nursing students' successful completion of nursing programs. There is still plenty of work to be done and to be shared among all educators. A survey participant wrote,

> As a white woman, there is more for me to learn, and I am trying to read more and be involved in strategic efforts to make a difference in identifying systemic racism and being both an ally and a co-conspirator (Administrator, Survey).

Meanings of Racism and the Lived Experience of Racism

Research Question 1 dealt with meanings of the lived experience of racism. Many meanings of racism for nursing educators at PWIs were discovered through qualitative online surveys and interview. The meanings of racism were explored along with other findings in Chapter IV of this dissertation. Findings for the meanings of racism were summarized there as falling into four major themes:

- Racism is Omnipresent and Insidious
- Racism is Painful and Uncomfortable
- Racism Denotes Ignorance and Lack of Knowledge
- Racism is Limiting

Racism is Omnipresent and Insidious. The findings of this study on the meanings of racism connect to existing literature on the omnipresence of racism. The first tenant of Critical Race Theory is that racism exists; racism is "normal" (Delgado & Stefancic, 2017, p. 8) and it is present everywhere. Many survey participants wrote about the presence of racism. Interview participants were less apt to define racism as being everywhere all the time, but most did say that they thought about racism in their daily work. There were two types of interview participants who were sure they thought about racism in their everyday work, those who said they thought about it because they tried to avoid making missteps that might be considered racist or insensitive, and those who were aware that their own lived experiences involved dodging the fiery darts of racism on a daily basis. These findings connect to assertions by Bell (2021) and Sumpter et al. (2023) that it cannot be assumed that nursing educators can remove themselves from their "identities as racialized or non-racialized beings (Bell, 2021, p. 2) just because they are going to administer, teach in, or support a nursing program. The assumption that individuals bring themselves—replete with their experiences, attitudes, and beliefs—to work is part of the rationale for this study's design. Learning the context within which nursing educators operate is crucial to creating inclusive teaching and learning environments.

Racism is Painful and Uncomfortable. A number of study participants described the pain of racism as a physical hurt or discomfort that can be inflicted upon someone and that lasts in a person's memory. Several participants associated racism being uncomfortable, particularly when describing how their lived experiences with racism. Uncomfortable lived experiences with racism included witnessing racism in the movies or in the news, seeing a colleague being treated differently, and being accused of being racist. The theme of racism being painful and uncomfortable is a new finding that was not discussed in the literature reviewed in Chapter II of this study. The literature reviewed did not include descriptions of physical pain. However, death related to racism was a theme. The death of George Floyd and the disparity in COVID-19 related deaths among racial/ethnic groups in America was covered in the literature review. A plethora of healthcare disparities and social injustices that lead to death may be attributed to racism in the U.S. (Iheduru-Anderson & Alexander, 2022; Matthews et al. 2022), including a COVID-19 mortality rate for African Americans that was two times the mortality rate of White Americans (Tai et al., 2021).

Racism Denotes Ignorance and Lack of Knowledge. Racism was defined by several participants as assumptions or judgments made without knowledge. More than one study participant expressed worry or fear that they might "unknowingly" contribute to racism or have something that could be construed as racist happen because of something they did or said. Worry is synonymous with fear (Thesaurus.com, 2024). Ignorance as a finding connects with the greater body of literature on racism and aligns with the CRT framework. Charles Mills (2007) defined not knowing, choosing not to acknowledge, or suppressing the truth about race as White ignorance. There were a few answers among this study's survey responses that said that racism was a thing of the past, that a participant had not noticed racism at their institution or experienced it in life, there was no need noted for special supports for Black students, or that avoidance was a strategy for addressing racism in nursing. They are enumerated in Chapter IV. The failure to recognize the need for support for this group of students expressed by the minority of participants in this study is not an unexpected finding. This finding agrees with the Chinn et al. (2022) assessment that nursing educators, particularly White nursing educators, may lack knowledge about racism, based on their personal patterns of knowing. Wesp et al. (2018) would caution that nursing educators' lack of understanding of the needs of Black nursing students contributes to the discrimination of these students.

Racism is Limiting. Findings that racism is limiting and creates barriers contributes to evidence from Harris et al. (2014) and Matthews et al. (2022). Those studies addressed attrition and the barriers Black nursing students faced that lead to attrition. An example from the White et al. (2020) study explained how mistrust limited communication among faculty and students. Similar accounts of miscommunication and mistrust were shared in the findings of this dissertation study by faculty who said they had been accused by students of being racist.

Systemic Racism. Racism was defined multiple ways by multiple individuals in this study. The word, "systemic" was used by six survey participants to define, describe, and discuss racism. Lily used the metaphor of cancer destroying bodily systems, explicitly using the words, "systems" and "structure" to define racism. Iris discussed a "system" associated with racism when she spoke about members of the community surrounding her institution who "didn't understand property and property value" sold their homes and were "victims of redlining". Fifteen percent of survey participants and 15% of interview participants addressed racism as a systematic or structural phenomenon. This study's participants' definitions of racism indicate their adherence to a more narrow definition of the meaning of racism than the Braveman et al. (2022) definition put forth in Chapter II of this study. Braveman et al. (2022) put forth that systemic racism "reflect[s] the natural, inevitable order of things" (Braveman et al., 2022, p. 172). This finding indicates that there is opportunity for further education among nursing educators on racism and its effects. This finding supports the incorporation of CRT into nursing curriculum to assure that nurses understand systemic and structural racism (Iheduru-Anderson & Alexander, 2022). The first tenet of CRT is applicable to this finding and its connection to the literature. Racism exists, is systemic, and is a normal, everyday phenomenon in the U.S. (Delgado & Stefancic, 2017).

Fear, Angry Black Woman, Playing the Race Card. Nursing educators' narratives of fear, the "angry Black woman," and "playing the race card" as meanings of the lived experience of racism as depicted in this dissertation study contrast with the body of literature on Black students' experiences at PWIs. These were unexpected findings that fell outside of the scope of the literature review conducted for this dissertation. Survey responses elaborated on how mislabeling Black students as angry adds to their difficulty navigating and belonging in the mostly White environment of a PWI. A survey showed that simply speaking with a different cadence from faculty and other students can be isolating for a Black student at a PWI.

The theme and descriptions of the "Angry Black Woman" shared in this dissertation study are not atypical of Black students' experiences at PWIs. In their study on the effects of racial battle fatigue on Black, biracial, and multiracial students graduate students, Ragland Woods et al. (2021) explained the stereotype of the angry, hostile, and aggressive Black student. Ragland Woods et al. (2021) told how Black students who responded to racial microaggressions by confronting their aggressors were labeled by the aggressors as "angry" and "combative" (Ragland Woods et al., 2021, p. 222). Ragland Woods et al. (2021) associated the "angry Black woman" trope with fear on the part of the aggressor, "Aggressors also may disengage from students to avoid fear and anxiety associated with committing another microaggression and/or being confronted on such an aggression-this defensive response has been described as White fragility and White silence" (Ragland Woods et al, 2021, p. 222).

Lily's narrative illustrated the ease with which one could potentially mislabel Black students, regardless of gender, as angry, and how she avoided making that mistake. Motro et al. (2022) defined the "angry Black woman" stereotype and warned against perpetuating it:

The pervasive ['angry Black woman'] stereotype…characterizes Black women as more

hostile, aggressive, overbearing, illogical, ill-tempered, and bitter… and [causes companies] to miss out on the full contribution of Black women in their organizations

because of this image (Motro et al., 2022, paras. 1-3).

Acknowledging biases, using empathy, and being intentional about challenging racial

stereotypes are ways to avoid labeling valuable contributors to an organization (Motro et al.,

2022).

Perceived Impacts of Racism on Black Nursing Students

Research Question 2 sought to discover nursing educators at PWIs' perceptions of the

impacts of racism on Black nursing students. Findings in this section are divided into two topics:

- Challenges faced by Black nursing students

- Support systems in place for Black nursing students.

The findings in this section were elicited by asking participants to identify support systems in

place for black nursing students at their institutions. Themes that emerged were

underrepresentation, differences or being a visible minority, being taught through a white lens,

lack of preparation, and friendship. The challenges faced by Black nursing students at PWIs as

perceived by the nursing educators in this study agree with findings from the larger body of

literature on the lived experiences of Black nursing students. Several studies reviewed in Chapter

II described challenges. They include Ackerman-Barger & Hummel (2015), Ackerman-Barger et

al. (2020), Attis-Josias (2023), Bell (2021), Childs et al. (2004), Harris et al. (2014), White &

Fulton (2015), and White et al. (2020).

Underrepresentation. In their 2014 study on attrition, Harris et al. found that "current

nursing programs…lack broad diversity in their student bodies… although minority nursing

student enrollment has grown, it is still not representative of the US population" (Harris et al.,

2014, p. 32). Several of the participants in this dissertation study attributed Black students' challenges to their being underrepresented at PWIs.

Being a Visible Minority & Being Taught Through a White Lens. Regarding the theme of being taught through a White lens, these findings correspond to discussions by Iheduru-Anderson and Alexander (2022) and Blythe Bell (2021), reviewed in Chapter II, about the dominance of Whiteness in nursing education. Bell (2021) goes into Eurocentrism, White privilege—which is mentioned by an interview participant in this study—and the lack of critical discussion of racism in nursing at length in her literature review. Ackerman-Barger and Hummel (2015) and Iheduru-Anderson and Alexander (2022) recommended examining the lens through which nursing education is approached and introducing CRT as a new perspective into nursing curricula. Iheduru-Anderson and Alexander (2022) discussed the centricity of Whiteness in nursing curricula and instruction.

Findings of this study indicated that there were not enough Black faculty at the participants' institutions to be role models for Black nursing students. White and Fulton (2015) found that several of the African American students in the studies they reviewed preferred role models from among nursing educators who they perceived struggled their own way through nursing school. The students in that study reported that African American role models were understanding of the students' experience. Unless students in the White and Fulton (2015) study found faculty to be approachable, they tended not to seek help from faculty.

Lack of Preparation. Several participants discussed their experiences with or perceptions of Black students' lack of preparation for nursing school, including survey participants, two administrators, and two faculty interviewed in this study. These findings align with broader literature reviewed in Chapter II of this dissertation. Dewsbury et al. (2022) and

Matthews et al. (2022) addressed limited preparation in STEM courses in their strategies for removing barriers to student success.

Friendships and Class. White and Fulton's (2015) findings agree with this dissertation study's findings that making friends with White classmates at a PWI is a challenge for Black students. White and Fulton (2015) affirmed that employment and family obligations were barriers to forming friendships in nursing school. Bell (2021) discussed class as a barrier to teaching antiracism in her study.

Support Systems for Black Nursing Students at PWIs

On Teaching Cultural Competency and Addressing Racism. Nursing educators participating in individual interviews for this dissertation study broached the topics of being culturally competent and teaching cultural competency without being specifically asked to do so. There was a wide range of responses in the surveys to how nursing educators address racism. Responses ran the gamut from racism being addressed in freshmen courses to the topic of racism being avoided. Closest to the center is the broader theme that there is room for improvement in this area. These findings, along with discussions by participants of this study about the power gradient between educators and students and how racism is addressed in nursing education are consistent with the literature reviewed in Chapter II of this study. Bell (2021) criticized nursing education for prioritizing a "culturalist approach to nursing across difference" (Bell, 2021, p. 3) over responding to the Eurocentricity of nursing education by teaching antiracism. Ackerman-Barger and Hummel (2015) and Iheduru-Anderson and Waite (2022) discussed the concepts of power and privilege as they relate to the inclusion of cultural competency in nursing curriculum.

Nurses Eat Their Young. This study's findings contribute to the literature on socialization into the profession and bullying (Dzurec, 2022), and corroborate with Iheduru-

Anderson and Alexander's (2022) assertion that nursing students are socialized into the profession through the hidden curriculum.

Support Systems. Findings indicated that support systems in place for Black nursing students are often administered by entities such as multicultural groups, directors of DEI, deans of inclusive excellence, and other administrators. Supports for Black students and efforts to address racism in nursing education sometimes reside within the same structures. An overwhelming number of responses indicated that deans and other administrators, DEI offices, affinity groups outside of nursing, and Black nursing educators bear the brunt of the responsibility for creating and maintaining structures that support Black nursing students at PWIs. Faculty and administrators interviewed for this study shared specific ways they supported Black students. They talked about supporting student-led events, mentoring, advocating, securing financing, and assuring students' emotional safety in the clinical setting. Findings from faculty, staff, and administrators' interviews and surveys regarding addressing racism in nursing education and supporting Black nursing students are congruent with findings from current literature on the topic (Eudy & Brooks, 2022; Henderson et al., 2020; Matthews et al., 2022).

Racial Battle Fatigue and Self-Care. Important to this study's findings that select individuals and systems are accountable for supporting Black students and for addressing racism is the potential that these resources may be in need of support themselves. Evidence from current scholarship shows that individuals coping with constant microaggressions, and other expressions of racism experienced real, visceral exhaustion. The cumulative physical, mental, and emotional effects of coping with racism lead to "racial battle fatigue" (Quaye et al., 2020, p.609; Ragland Woods et al., 2021, p. 221) Quaye et al. (2020) described racial battle fatigue as affecting not only those racialized individuals who live daily with the stressors of racism, but also those individuals who work to combat and eradicate racism. Racial battle fatigue was expressed by participants in the Quaye et al. (2020) study as "a physical battle; hyperalertness; suppressed rage; and emotional, mental, and physical exhaustion. This exhaustion was manifested in participants' everyday work" (Quaye et al., 2020, p. 616). Quaye et al. (2020) asserted that the expectation that students and educators experiencing racial battle fatigue would practice "self-care" while trying to survive in "larger systems of oppression" (Quaye et al., 2020, p. 610) was mere rhetoric.

This dissertation study's findings around addressing racism and support for Black nursing students also connect with the literature reviewed in Chapter II that discussed to need for educators to acknowledge and embrace their responsibility to eliminate the academic achievement gap that often lies between White students and students from historically disenfranchised groups (Dewsbury et al., 2022). Additionally, according to the broader body of literature, educators are accountable for preparing all their students socially for the role of the registered nurse. This entails mentoring, role-modeling, and instilling professional values (Salisu et al., 2019). As Violet stated in her interview, "there is absolutely a need for us to do better." Doing better is a mandate for *all* nursing educators.

Broad Themes

Two broad and overarching themes, gathered by looking and listening deeply and intently and reflexively throughout the process of this study, are Awareness and Communication.

Awareness

One hundred percent of nursing educators who participated in the study were cognizant of the existence—past or present—of racism in our society and in nursing education. There was an awareness expressed by most participants in surveys and interviews that Black students faced challenges at PWIs that were different from, if not greater than, the challenges that White students faced at PWIs. These findings contradict findings from broader literature (Eudy & Brooks, 2022; Green, 2020; Tobbell, 2023) which reasons that nursing educators may not understand the challenges racism presents for their Black students. The nursing educators in this dissertation study understood many, although not all the challenges faced by their Black nursing students. This lack of full awareness is evident in the findings around "angry Black woman" and "playing the race card." This study's findings indicate that only a small number (15%) of study participants expressed an understanding of the systemic and structural foundations of racism. Lack of understanding of the systemic nature of racism by nursing educators was covered in studies by Bell (2021) and Dancis and Coleman (2022). The failure to see racism as systemic intersects with prioritizing teaching cultural competency over teaching antiracism and with the third tenet of CRT which lays out the social construction of racism (Delgado & Stefancic, 2017; Iheduru-Anderson & Alexander, 2022).

Communication

Considering the unexpected findings of this study, "angry Black woman, and "playing the race card", there may be a disconnect between nursing educators at PWIs and their Black nursing students caused primarily by miscommunication or lack of communication. These findings indicate that Black nursing students at PWIs may receive messages and interpret messages communicated by educators one way and nursing educators at PWIs may think the messages they send are received and interpreted perhaps another way. Literature related to nursing students' and educators' inability to separate their academic and professional selves from the social and historical contexts in which they dwell (Bell, 2021; Sumpter et al., 2023) aligns with the theme of failure to communicate that this researcher extrapolates from the findings of this study. Evidence from the interviews conducted for this dissertation study show that educators' background, personal experiences, and perceptions are part of their lived experience with racism. The findings of this dissertation study present the counternarratives of nursing educators at PWIs as a contrast to the narratives of Black nursing students shared in the broader literature. The counternarratives, as they are viewed through the lens of Critical Race Theory, told in this dissertation study amplify the voices of nursing educators at PWIs, whose stories have not been well-documented in current literature, and illuminate the need for better communication between nursing educators and Black nursing students at PWIs.

Limitations

The use of online qualitative surveys might be seen by some readers as a limitation. Responses to survey questions, particularly those asking for meanings, may have been copied and pasted from dictionaries or textbooks. This researcher reminds the reader that the type of survey used for this study was a qualitative, not quantitative data collection instrument. Whether participants wrote original thoughts or canned responses, the narratives told here represent the voices of the participants. The researcher did not seek verifiability in this phenomenological study, but rather sought to explore the meanings of the phenomenon of racism and perceptions by educators at PWIs of the impact of racism on Black nursing students.

The researcher's positionality may have been a limitation to participation in this study. The researcher speculated that because she is Black faculty, many of the colleagues (of all races and ethnicities) with whom she shared the study invitation assumed that Black nursing faculty were the target population for this study. A few people who responded to e-mail or social media invitations said that they would share the invitation with the colleagues they knew worked in the diversity, equity, and inclusion (DEI) area of their institution. The researcher checked the language and tone of the study invitations and posted on social media three times, each time using different language to attempt to make clear the purpose of the study and the intended participants.

Staff responses to invitations to the study were sparse. This challenge was consistent with the lack of data on staff or nursing programs. Most staff were recruited to participate in interviews in-person by the researcher. One staff member told the researcher that they usually deleted email invitations to research studies because, in their experience, research studies hardly ever applied to staff. Some staff expressed concern about confidentiality during their interviews and may not have shared to the extent they would have because of their lack of familiarity and possible mistrust with participating in a qualitative research study.

Implications

A few survey participants expressed an interest in or necessity to learn more about the topic of racism and its effects on Black nursing students. One hoped that the researcher would "learn a lot and use the data to better support nursing students." Several individuals expressed, in written survey responses or verbally at the end of their interviews, their interest in learning the outcome of the study and their hopes that there would be some sort of action as a result of this study. As was established in the Significance section of Chapter I of this study, by documenting the meanings of the lived experience of racism for nursing educators at PWIs, this study adds to existing knowledge about nursing educators' roles in preparing future nurses. This dissertation study is significant as it engaged participants in considering the meanings of racism and expressions of racism in nursing education, and it engaged participants in thinking about the impact of racism on the Black nursing students at their institutions. The purpose of this study was to gain an understanding of nursing educators at PWIs' meanings of racism their perceptions of the effects of racism on Black nursing students. Perhaps through this exploration of the meanings effects of racism, there will be a broader understanding among nursing educators that racism affects everyone. This study addresses the paucity of literature on the topic of racism and gives scholars data with which to compare the lived experiences of nursing educators and the lived experiences of Black nursing students at PWIs as they were explored in Chapter II of this study.

Recommendations

Recommendations for Practice

The relationship between this study's findings and themes from the literature reviewed in Chapters I and II of this study may be of interest to nursing education scientists, nursing administrators, faculty, and staff of nursing education programs. Understanding the perspectives of nursing educators may be beneficial in developing strategies for not only retaining but also recruiting nursing students of color. Discovering that nursing educators' meanings of racism and their perceptions of the challenges faced by Black nursing students at PWIs are consistent with reports from the larger body of literature about Black nursing students' experiences at PWIs is both helpful and hopeful. Understanding the contrast between what nursing educators think they know about racism and how they think they are providing support to Black nursing students and the lived experiences of Black nursing students may serve as a basis for reimagining nursing education through the lens of CRT as suggested by Iheduru-Anderson and Alexander (2022).

Viewing this study through the lens of CRT, the researcher considers that there may be a gap between how educators think they are helping and what Black students believe that they actually receive as help. The data obtained in this dissertation study suggests that the participants represented here believe their nursing programs and the larger institutions to which they belong believe their environments are, or aim to be, diverse, equitable, and inclusive. This is regardless

of the terminology used to describe DEI efforts or the extent to which those efforts are

measurable and successful. Considering the data and recommendations graciously shared by the

participants of this study, this researcher suggests that nursing program administrators lead this

charge: Demonstrate your nursing program's commitment to equity and inclusion by

encouraging increased communication among nursing educators and students, and by adopting

practices that are more considerate and inclusive of Black nursing students. Perhaps, as a result,

the experience of Black nursing students will be considered by nursing education leaders seeking

concrete solutions to alleviate the nursing shortage and to add to the diversity of the nursing

workforce. Recommendations for future practice are

1. Institute face-to-face group "check-in" sessions between nursing educators and Black

   nursing students at the beginning of each school year and periodically to set expectations

   and communicate strategic plans for the prescribed time period. The data from this study

   suggests that nursing educators can do a better job of communicating with students to

   learn students' perspectives and to share resources with students. Data from this study

   also suggests that first-generation students and first-year students generally require

   substantial support and guidance.

2. Require individual exit interviews between students and nursing program administrators

   to better learn about the challenges students faced in the program and the supports that

   worked and resources that were lacking. Data from this study shows that there is a power

   gradient between educators and students. Speaking with students who have completed the

   program before they leave the institution gives a current student perspective and flattens

   the power gradient as students transition to graduates. Exit interviews may provide valuable information for program administrators that may be given immediate consideration. Exit interviews also give educators the opportunity to send graduates into the workforce with words of encouragement that demonstrate that new graduates are welcomed in the profession. None of the participants in this study discussed bridging the gap between student and practicing nurse among challenges or supports. The researcher's personal experience is that encouragement from educators was memorable and contributed to building her resilience while working in challenging situations. Encouragement from educators across every level of the researcher's pre-licensure program (program chair, faculty, and staff— at a community college), while she was a nursing student, encouraged her to pursue advanced nursing education and become a nursing educator within five years of graduation from nursing school. Encouraging nursing graduates to become educators is key to alleviating the nursing shortage.

3. Invite all soon-to-be graduates to group debriefing sessions as requirements for graduation. In interviews and group debriefing sessions, educators would be required to not only speak, but also listen to Black nursing students. Educators could use a script with prompts, like those used in an employment interview or a qualitative research interview, to build rapport and encourage conversation. The script or questionnaire should inquire about the students' lived experiences as Black students in the nursing program, which supports provided by the nursing program were helpful and how those supports addressed the students' challenges, and what supports the students thought should be maintained or improved to make Black students feel like they belonged in the nursing program and in the nursing profession. Holding listening sessions, or exit-interviews, for all students – not just Black students - might yield a wealth of information for program

administrators. Additionally, requiring all students to participate will assure that students

of color do not feel singled out.

4. Form a committee of administrators, faculty and staff tasked with attending and

   facilitating interviews, group sessions, and compiling results. Membership on this

   committee should be a mix of people from within the nursing program (junior staff, full

   professors, non-tenured, adjuncts, etc.) and could be rotated every year or two so that all

   educators have the opportunity to serve. Committee members should receive preparation

   to facilitate sessions with students from diversity, equity, inclusion, and belonging

   (DEIB) professionals, with certification and expertise in their subject areas, consulted

   from outside of the nursing program. Data from this dissertation study indicated that the

   individuals responsible for implementing DEI initiatives at some of the participants'

   institutions did not have a professional background and qualifications to administer DEI

   programs. Data also indicated that not all educators were doing DEI work. It is the

   position of this researcher that the work of assuring an equitable, inclusive teaching and

   learning environment where everyone feels supported is everyone's work.

5. The next part of the strategy to adopt more inclusive practices involves requiring all

   nursing educators, administrators, faculty, and staff of a nursing program to work together

   to review and code the data from the sessions described above come up with themes.

   Those themes might be further explored for feasibility for incorporation into curricula,

   policies, and practice. Then, doable interventions should be implemented immediately

   and reviewed on a regular basis. Similar to using the nursing process to create a nursing

   care plan for an individual or a group, nursing program educators are encouraged to

   collaborate to create a care plan for a more inclusive nursing program. Leaders from among administrators and seasoned and tenured faculty are challenged to take up this

charge and show their less-seasoned colleagues the way.

6. Racial battle fatigue as it affects Black students and the educators supporting them should

be considered by leadership. Tangible resources to care for affected students and

educators can be incorporated into the culture of nursing programs. Individuals suffering

racial battle fatigue cannot be expected to effectively care for themselves in environments

where they are unsupported by administration. This researcher has observed caring

measures, during her career, that can be incorporated into strategic planning. These

include allowing students and educators to take personal/mental health days off, social

gatherings that include food and music, field trips, nature walks, and spaces for gathering.

Recommendations for Future Research

Hearing from a diverse group of nursing educators was valuable and resulted in rich data.

A recommendation for future research is that a larger number of educators from diverse

backgrounds be included and that demographic questions ask about regions, type, and size of

representative institutions. It was not the intent of this study to learn only from one racial or

ethnic group. However, a recommendation for future study is focusing solely on the lived

experiences of White female nursing faculty, as they are the majority group in nursing education.

Additionally, exploring the experiences of White nursing educators at HBCUs, minority-serving

institutions and other nursing programs where the student body is diverse may add a different

perspective to current knowledge on the lived experiences of nursing educators. Future research

might explore nursing educators' specific, individual practices that support and encourage Black

nursing students to complete nursing school and that ease the transition to nursing practice.

Additional recommendations for future study include utilizing qualitative online surveys to explore inclusive teaching methodologies in nursing classroom, clinical, and laboratory settings. A quantitative study is recommended to discover the extent to which nursing educators employ inclusive practices in their teaching.

A Narrative for Nursing Education. As the end of this dissertation study drew near, and the researcher thought broadly about it, she felt the urge to consider the study's findings within the CRT tradition of storytelling. Storytelling and narratives are a way of "opening a window onto ignored or alternative realities" (Delgado & Stefancic, 2017, p. 46). A summary of this study would be incomplete without a narrative. This narrative will be told in first-person, as it was seen in a dream by the researcher. I see the current state of nursing education in the following imaginary scene: Delivery trucks drop off goods to small businesses with limited space for loading and unloading cargo. These large, box trucks double-park on narrow city streets and squeeze into alleyways carved out long ago that were never meant for motorized vehicles. Upstairs residents would rather endure the stifling heat of the indoors than open their windows to the noise and odor of diesel engines idling outside the downstairs businesses. Walkers who venture outside of their havens during the endless deliveries of the day sidestep pools of spills and tiptoe across rutted walkways, all the while hoping not to be clobbered by passing vehicular traffic as they slide their way around the cabs of trucks jutting out into the street. Shoppers squeeze in and out of the little spaces left by drivers who maneuver handcarts and deposit wares at counters and in busy doorways. Drops complete, the drivers make their way out of those tight, dank places and continue onto their next stops.

Considering the implications of this study for the future of nursing education, I compare what I considers to be standard operating procedures in nursing education to getting goods and services in and out of narrow streets (standard operating procedures in nursing might include those lessons found within the hidden or implicit curriculum; examples are lectures with wordy slides, daytime classes and practica for working adult students, and requirements that self-expressions of tattoos and facial piercings be covered in the clinical setting). I wonder if the streets could be widened to allow traffic to maneuver around the parked trucks. Then I think, instead, that maybe it is not the streets that need updating, but the delivery process. The process of supplying the community with necessities could be streamlined, with deliveries by truck being limited to a certain time window each day. If we are limited by space and resources, must we also be limited by time? Replacing unnecessary vehicle traffic with bicycle couriers for smaller deliveries would also help alleviate the bottleneck of traffic caused by the trucks. Streamlining operations would require including business owners, truckers, consumers, and residents of the neighborhood to communicate and cooperate to solve their common problem. Working together to free up the space they all share by limiting, but optimizing, delivery times might result in room for recreational activities like walking, skating, biking, sidewalk café dining, and entertainment that could be enjoyed by everyone. Consumers would continue to have access to the goods and services they needed. Everyone would benefit from a reimagined system. I imagine how much more beautiful the days would seem to business owners and residents, and how truckers would experience less stress when visiting a cramped neighborhood with a process that was understood and embraced by all the constituents.

In this vision, there is no entity in my narrative that I associate directly with any of the characters in the real world of nursing education. But what I see is that nursing educators, like the truckers and the business owners and the residents in my imaginary story, are experts at their routines, for they have practiced them for a long time. They manage their roles and do what they do well. If the process was not working for them, they would not still be following it. Everything works the way everyone believes things were intended to work. Or, at least, everything works the way everyone has known things to always work. The process is not broken. However, the process could be better. And there are underlying issues that affect everyone in the long term in my imaginary story that could very easily remain unseen as long as people and processes continue to move along as usual. Perhaps a newcomer to the neighborhood points out the problems or potential problems in my imaginary story; perhaps a resident of the community travels and sees that people in a similar community enjoy times during the day where they can open their windows and air out their apartments and they can let their children play on the sidewalk in the afternoon after school because deliveries are done for the day and the sidewalks have been cleared. The resident had not realized what was missing from her neighborhood until she visited someone else's. A world of opportunity in nursing education awaits once the window onto "alternative realities" (Delgado & Stefancic, 2017, p. 46) has been opened.

The Impetus to Conduct this Study

This study is timely. For the sake of space and time, all the reasons why this study is timely are not written here. A review of Chapter II. Review of the Literature may help the reader with the timeliness and relevance of this study. The reader is encouraged to refresh their knowledge of current events, particularly during the period from 2020 to 2024, related to the intersection of racism and political polarization in the U.S. with the COVID-19 pandemic and attacks on higher education. The researcher saw a need for action— aimed at institutions who value their Black students and want to retain them (in light of the recent SCOTUS decision to reverse Affirmative Action) and at nursing educators, particularly leaders, who may not yet realize that failing to get students to graduation contributes to the nursing shortage and will have detrimental long-term effects. The researcher desired to contribute scholarship to the science of nursing education that could be translated to immediate action.

This study was time limited. This dissertation study was conducted as Cabrini University prepared to close its doors for the last time. This was a bittersweet time for students, staff, and faculty alike. Cabrini University was a hidden gem, where the mission, which included Mother Cabrini's vision of "education of the heart" (Cabrini University, n.d., p. 1) and a commitment to social justice, were actualized through teaching and learning, scholarship, and service. Once this researcher decided to pursue a doctorate in higher education leadership, it did not take much deliberation to settle on the graduate program at Cabrini University. The program was academically rigorous yet affordable. The cohort model offered in-person and synchronous online courses and allowed students to build on our professional networks. The instruction was top-notch. The commitment to social justice meant that students could choose dissertation topics that would not only add values-based scholarship to the body of literature in our disciplines, but also inform real-world practice and be informed by our real-life experiences (mine being that of a Black woman in nursing education). Having Cabrini University close before this dissertation study was completed would have meant starting from scratch with a new study on a less-sensitive topic, or defending my rationale for studying issues of race and racism to a new set of faculty and administrators who just might not have understood. These considerations motivated this researcher to take the option to stay at Cabrini and accelerate my studies, fitting what was originally intended to be a three-year program into two years. Because the faculty was willing to stay the course, so was I. As we close the book on Cabrini University I am full of gratitude and hope, optimistic for the rest of this story that remains to be written.

References

Aaron, D. G., Bajaj, S. S., & Stanford, F. C. (2023). Supreme Court cases on affirmative action threaten diversity in medicine. *Proceedings of the National Academy of Sciences, 120*(17), e2220919120. https://doi.org/10.1073/pnas.2220919120

Ackerman-Barger, K., Boatright, D., Gonzalez-Colaso, R., Orozco, R., & Latimore, D. (2020). Seeking inclusion excellence: Understanding racial microaggressions as experienced by underrepresented medical and nursing students. *Academic Medicine, 95*(5), 758. https://doi.org/10.1097/ACM.0000000000003077

Ackerman-Barger, K., & Hummel, F. (2015). Critical Race Theory as a lens for exploring inclusion and equity in nursing education. *Journal of Theory Construction & Testing, 19*(2), 39-46.

Adams, C. (2021, May 10). How Trump ignited the fight over Critical Race Theory in schools. *NBC News.* https://www.nbcnews.com/news/nbcblk/how-trump-ignited-fight-over-critical-race-theory-schools-n1266701

Adeniran, R., Jones, D., Harmon, M., Hexem-Hubbard, S. & Gonzalez, E. (2023). Checking the pulse of holistic and culturally competent nursing practice in Pennsylvania. *Holistic Nursing Practice, 37*(4), 223-232. https://doi.org/10.1097/HNP.0000000000000427

Aebersold, M. (2018). Simulation-based learning: No longer a novelty in undergraduate education. *OJIN: The Online Journal of Issues in Nursing, 23*(2). https://doi.org/10.3912/OJIN.Vol23No02PPT39

Akamine Phillips, J., Risdon, N., Lamsma, M., Hambrick, A., & Jun, A. (2019). Barriers and strategies by white faculty who incorporate anti-racist pedagogy. *Race and Pedagogy*

Journal: Teaching and Learning for Justice, 3(2), 1.

https://soundideas.pugetsound.edu/rpj/vol3/iss2/1

Alexander, M. (2018). Foreword. In D. Bell. *Faces at the bottom of the well: The permanence of racism* (pp. ix-xix). Basic Books.

Allcorn, S. (2021). White supremacy and the pursuit of power. *Journal of Psychohistory, 48*(4), 277-289. https://psycnet.apa.org/record/2021-40233-002

Alsan, M., Garrick, O., & Graziani, G. C. (2019). Does diversity matter for health? Experimental evidence from Oakland. *American Economic Review, 109*(12), 4071-4111. https://www.aeaweb.org/articles?id=10.1257/aer.20181446

American Association of Colleges of Nursing. (2019). *AACN's vision for academic nursing.* https://www.aacnnursing.org/Portals/0/PDFs/White-Papers/Vision-Academic-Nursing.pdf

American Association of Colleges of Nursing. (2021). *The essentials: Core competencies for professional nursing education.* https://www.aacnnursing.org/Portals/0/PDFs/Publications/Essentials-2021.pdf

American Association of Colleges of Nursing. (2023a). *Diversity, equity, & inclusion: An AACN faculty toolkit. Glossary.* https://www.aacnnursing.org/diversity-tool-kit/glossary

American Association of Colleges of Nursing. (2023b). *Nursing workforce fact sheet.* https://www.aacnnursing.org/news-data/fact-sheets/nursing-workforce

American Council on Education. (2023). *Carnegie classification of institutions of higher education.* https://carnegieclassifications.acenet.edu/

American Nurses Association. (n.d.-a). *The nursing process.* https://www.nursingworld.org/practice-policy/workforce/what-is-nursing/the-nursing-process/

American Nurses Association. (n.d.-b). *What is nursing?* https://www.nursingworld.org/practice-policy/workforce/what-is-nursing/

American Psychological Association. (2020). *Publication manual of the American Psychological Association* (7th ed.). https://doi.org/10.1037/0000165-000

American Psychological Association. (2023). *Inclusive language guide* (2nd ed.). https://www.apa.org/about/apa/equity-diversity-inclusion/language-guidelines.pdf

Attis-Josias, M. (2023, June 29). BIPOC nursing students' perceived barriers to help-seeking when under stress. *Nursing Forum, (Vol. 2023)*, 1-7. https://doi.org/10.1155/2023/5977511

Basile, V., & Black, R. (2019). They hated me till I was one of the "good ones": Toward understanding and disrupting the differential racialization of undergraduate African American STEM majors. *The Journal of Negro Education, 88*(3), 379–390. https://doi.org/10.7709/jnegroeducation.88.3.0379

Bell, B. (2021). White dominance in nursing education: A target for anti-racist efforts. *Nursing Inquiry*, 28(1), e12379. https://doi.org/10.1111/nin.12379

Bell, D. (1992). *Faces.at the bottom of the well: The permanence of racism.* Basic Books.

Bell, D. (2018). *Faces at the bottom of the well: The permanence of racism.* Basic Books. (Original work published 1992)

Bell, D. A. (1995a). Brown v. Board of Education and the interest convergence dilemma. In K. Crenshaw, N. Gotanda, G. Peller, & K. Thomas (Eds.), *Critical race theory: The key writings that formed the movement* (pp. 21-29). The New Press.

Bell, D. A. (1995b). Serving two masters: Integration ideals and client interests in school desegregation litigation. In K. Crenshaw, N. Gotanda, G. Peller, & K. Thomas (Eds.),

Critical race theory: The key writings that formed the movement (pp. 5-19). The New Press.

Berman, A. (2015). Academic leadership development: A case study. *Journal of Professional Nursing, 31*(4), 298-304. https://doi.org/10.1016/j.profnurs.2015.02.006

Bjerkvik, L. K., & Hilli, Y. (2019). Reflective writing in undergraduate clinical nursing education: A literature review. *Nurse Education in Practice, 35*, 32-41. https://doi.org/10.1016/j.nepr.2018.11.013

Blanchet Garneau, A., Browne, A. J., & Varcoe, C. (2018). Drawing on antiracist approaches toward a critical antidiscriminatory pedagogy for nursing. *Nursing Inquiry, 25*(1), e12211. https://doi.org/10.1111/nin.12211

Booth, T. L., Emerson, C. J., Hackney, M. G., & Souter, S. (2016). Preparation of academic nurse educators. *Nurse Education in Practice, 19*, 54-57. https://doi.org/10.1016/j.nepr.2016.04.006

Borowsky, H. M., Willis, A., Bullock, J. L., Fuentes-Afflick, E., & Palmer, N. R. (2023). Opportunities and challenges in discussing racism during primary care visits. *Health Services Research, 58*(2), 282-290. https://doi-org/10.1111/1475-6773.14118

Boston College. Teaching writing. (2021). *Teaching the hidden curriculum: Inclusive teaching guides and tips.* https://www.bu.edu/teaching-writing/resources/teaching-the-hidden-curriculum/

Boswell, C. & Cannon, S. (2016a). Connection between evidence-based practice and nursing education. In S. Cannon & C. Boswell (Eds.), *Evidence-based teaching in nursing: A foundation for educators* (2nd ed., pp. 129-154). Jones & Bartlett Learning.

Boswell, C. & Cannon, S. (2016b). Overview of evidence-based practice. In S. Cannon & C.

Boswell (Eds.), *Evidence-based teaching in nursing: A foundation for educators* (2nd ed.,

pp. 1-29). Jones & Bartlett Learning.

Bouie, J. (2023, July 7). No one can stop talking about Justice John Marshall Harlan. *The New

York Times.* https://www.nytimes.com/2023/07/07/opinion/harlan-thomas-roberts-

affirmative-action.html

Bouws, M. R., Candela, L., & Bonnema, J. (2016). The novice nursing dean: A qualitative study

of the lived experience. *Journal of Nursing Education and Practice, 6*(8), 43-51.

https://www.sciedupress.com/journal/index.php/jnep/article/view/8358

Bouws, M., Madeira, A., & Streberger, A. (2020). Fulfillment in the role of academic nurse

leader: A grounded theory study. *Journal of Professional Nursing, 36*(6), 469-476.

https://doi.org/10.1016/j.profnurs.2020.03.007

Braun, V., & Clarke, V. (2006). Using thematic analysis in psychology. *Qualitative research in

psychology, 3*(2), 77-101. https://doi.org/10.1191/1478088706QP063OA

Braun, V., & Clarke, V. (2024). Thematic analysis. In N. K. Denzin, Y. S. Lincoln, M. D.

Giardina, & G. S. Cannella (Eds.), *The SAGE handbook of qualitative research* (6th ed.)

(pp. 385-402). SAGE.

Braun, V., Clarke, V., Boulton, E., Davey, L., & McEvoy, C. (2021). The online survey as a

qualitative research tool. *International journal of social research methodology, 24*(6),

641-654. https://doi.org/10.1080/13645579.2020.1805550

Braveman, P. A., Arkin, E., Proctor, D., Kauh, T., & Holm, N. (2022). Systemic and structural

racism: Definitions, examples, health damages, and approaches to dismantling. *Health

Affairs, 41*(2), 171-178. https://doi.org/10.1377/hlthaff.2021.01394

Brown University. (2015, February 27). *Kimberlé Crenshaw: Race today: A symposium on race in America. Race, gender, inequality and intersectionality*, [Video]. YouTube. https://www.youtube.com/watch?v=KNKbGFoYC1Q

Cabrini University. (n.d.). *Creating an Inclusive Campus: The Cabrini University statement of inclusivity. Inclusivity and Cabrini University mission.* https://www.cabrini.edu/globalassets/pdfs-website/wolfington/cabrini-university-statement-of-inclusivity.pdf

Cabrini University. (2024). *Cabrini University Dissertation Handbook*. Cabrini University.

Campaign for Action. (2023). *Increasing diversity in nursing. The nursing workforce should reflect the country's rich cultural and ethnic diversity.* https://campaignforaction.org/issue/increasing-diversity-in-nursing/

Caravelis, C., Harris, J. B., & Johnson, T. C. (2023). Crisis management. In K. Powers & P. J. Schloss (Eds.), *Organization and administration in higher education* (3rd ed., pp. 230-258). Routledge.

Carter, N., Bryant-Lukosius, D., DiCenso, A., Blythe, J., & Neville, A. J. (2014). The use of triangulation in qualitative research. *Oncology Nursing Forum, 41*(5), 545-7. https://doi.org/10.1188/14

Carter, B. M., & Phillips, B. C. (2021). Revolutionizing the nursing curriculum. *Creative Nursing, 27*(1), 25-30. https://doi.org/10.1891/CRNR-D-20-00072

Cary, M. P., Jr., Randolph, S. D., Broome, M. E., & Carter, B. M. (2020, November). Creating a culture that values diversity and inclusion: An action-oriented framework for schools of nursing. *Nursing Forum, 55*(4), 687-694. https://doi.org/10.1111/nuf.12485

Centers for Disease Control and Prevention. (2023 Aug 28). *CDC declares racism a public health threat*. https://www.cdc.gov/minorityhealth/racism-disparities/expert-perspectives/threat/index.html

Chen, H., Jensen, F., Chung, J., & Measom, G. (2020). Exploring faculty perceptions of teaching cultural competence in nursing. *Teaching and Learning in Nursing, 15*(1), 1-6. https://doi.org/10.1016/j.teln.2019.08.003

Childs, G., Jones, R., Nugent, K. E., & Cook, P. (2004). Retention of African-American students in baccalaureate nursing programs: Are we doing enough? *Journal of Professional Nursing, 20*(2), 129-133. https://doi.org/10.1016/j.profnurs.2004.03.002

Chinn, P. L., Kramer, M. K., & Sitzman, K. (2022). *Knowledge development in nursing: Theory and process* (11th ed.). Elsevier.

Clayton, A. B., McClay, L. P., Davis, R. D. & Tevis, T. L. (2023). Considering both HBCU and PWI options: Exploring the college choice process of first-year Black students. *The Journal of Higher Education, 94*(1), 34-59. https://doi.org/10.1080/00221546.2022.2131966

Crenshaw, K. (1995). Mapping the margins: Intersectionality, identity politics, and violence against women of color. In K. Crenshaw, N. Gotanda, G. Peller, & K. Thomas (Eds). *Critical race theory: The key writings that formed the movement* (pp. 357-383). The New Press.

Crenshaw, K., Gotanda, N., Peller, G., & Thomas, K. (Eds). (1995). *Critical race theory: The key writings that formed the movement*. The New Press.

Creswell, J. W., & Poth, C. N. (2018). *Qualitative inquiry & research design: Choosing among five approaches* (4th ed.). SAGE publications, Inc.

Culyer, L. M., Jatulis, L. L., Cannistraci, P., & Brownell, C. A. (2018). Evidenced-based teaching strategies that facilitate transfer of knowledge between theory and practice: what are nursing faculty using? *Teaching and Learning in Nursing, 13*(3), 174-179. https://doi.org/10.1016/j.teln.2018.03.003

Dancis, J., & Coleman, B. R. (2022). Transformative dissonant encounters: Opportunities for cultivating antiracism in White nursing students. *Nursing Inquiry, 29*(1), 1-14. https://doi.org/10.1111/nin.12447

Data USA. (2023). *Explore, map, compare, and download U.S. data.* https://datausa.io/

Davis, S., & O'Brien, A. M. (2020). Let's talk about racism: Strategies for building structural competency in nursing. *Academic Medicine, 95*(12S), S58-S65. https://doi.org/10.1097/ACM.0000000000003688

Delgado, R., & Stefancic, J. (2017). *Critical race theory: An introduction* (3rd ed.). New York University Press.

Denzin, N. K. (1970). *The research act: A theoretical introduction to sociological methods.* Aldine Publishing Company.

Denzin, N. K., Lincoln, Y. S., Giardina, M. D., & Cannella, G. S. (2024). Introduction: The discipline and practice of qualitative research. In N. K. Denzin, Y. S. Lincoln, M. D. Giardina, & G. S. Cannella (Eds.), *The SAGE handbook of qualitative research* (6th ed.) (pp. 1-27). SAGE.

Dewsbury, B. M., Swanson, H. J., Moseman-Valtierra S., & Caulkins, J. (2022) Inclusive and active pedagogies reduce academic outcome gaps and improve long-term performance. *PLoS ONE, 17*(6): e0268620. https://doi.org/10.1371/journal.pone.0268620

DeZure, D., Shaw, A., & Rojewski, J. (2014). Cultivating the next generation of academic leaders: Implications for administrators and faculty. *Change: The Magazine of Higher Learning, 46*(1), 6-12. https://doi.org/10.1080/00091383.2013.842102

Dillard-Wright, J., Valderama-Wallace, C., Canty, L., Perron, A., De Sousa, I., & Gullick, J. (2023). What nursing chooses not to know: Practices of epistemic silence/silencing. *Nursing Philosophy, 24*(3), e12443. https://doi.org/10.1111/nup.12443

District of Columbia Office of Racial Equity. (2022). *Guide to inclusive language: Race and ethnicity*. District of Columbia Office of Human Rights https://ohr.dc.gov/sites/default/files/dc/sites/ohr/page_content/attachments/OHR_ILG_RaceEthnicity_FINAL%20%281%29.pdf

The Divine Names. (2022, June 16). *Cornel West explains critical race theory* [Video]. YouTube. https://youtu.be/AftoggVdQwY?si=ssbQ4-OMxJ5LvxQs

Donnor, J. K., & Billings-Ladson, G. (2024). Critical race theory and the postracial imaginary. In N. K. Denzin, Y. S. Lincoln, M. D. Giardina, & G. S. Cannella (Eds.), *The SAGE handbook of qualitative research* (6th ed., pp. 385-402). SAGE.

Douglas, M. K., Rosenkoetter, M., Pacquiao, D. F., Callister, L. C., Hattar-Pollara, M., Lauderdale, J., Milstead, J., Nardi, D., & Purnell, L. (2014). Guidelines for implementing culturally competent nursing care. *Journal of Transcultural Nursing, 25*(2), 109-121. https://doi.org/10.1177/1043659614520

Duman, B. (2023). Metaphors on the null curriculum. *International Online Journal of Education and Teaching (IOJET), 10*(4). 2274-2286.

Dzurec, L. (2022). Storytelling and workplace bullying as deterrents to evidence-based innovation in teaching: Nurse educators' lived experiences. *Nursing Education Perspectives, 43*(1), 5-10. https://doi.org/10.1097/01.NEP.0000000000000900

Emerson, R. J., & Records, K. (2008). Today's challenge, tomorrow's excellence: The practice of evidence-based education. *Journal of Nursing Education, 47*(8), 359-370. https://doi.org/10.3928/01484834-20080801-04

Eudy, C., & Brooks, S. (2022). Factors impacting student success in a fundamentals course of an associate degree nursing program. *Teaching and Learning in Nursing, 17*(1), 11-16. https://doi.org/10.1016/j.teln.2021.05.004

Fitzgerald, A., McNelis, A. M., & Billings, D. M. (2020). NLN Core Competencies for nurse educators: Are they present in the course descriptions of academic nurse educator programs? *Nursing Education Perspectives, 41*(1), 4-9. https://doi.org/10.1097/01.NEP.0000000000000530

Fressola, M. C., & Patterson, G. E. (2017). *Transition from clinician to educator: A practical approach.* Jones & Bartlett Learning.

Fusch, P., Fusch, G. E., & Ness, L. R. (2018). Denzin's paradigm shift: Revisiting triangulation in qualitative research. *Journal of Sustainable Social Change, 10*(1), 2. https://doi.org/10.5590/JOSC.2018.10.1.02

Ghasemi, M. R., Moonaghi, H. K., & Heydari, A. (2020). Strategies for sustaining and enhancing nursing students' engagement in academic and clinical settings: A narrative review. *Korean Journal of Medical Education, 32*(2), 103–117. https://doi.org/10.3946/kjme.2020.159

Gotanda, N. (1995). A critique of "Our constitution is color-blind". In K. Crenshaw, N. Gotanda, G. Peller, & K. Thomas (Eds.), *Critical race theory: The key writings that formed the movement* (pp. 257-275). The New Press.

Green, C. (2020). Equity and diversity in nursing education. *Teaching and Learning in Nursing, 15*(4), 280–283. https://doi.org/10.1016/j.teln.2020.07.004

Green, A., & Ridenour, N. (2004). Shaping a career trajectory in academic administration: Leadership development for the deanship. *Journal of Nursing Education, 43*(11), 489-495. https://doi.org/10.3928/01484834-20041101-04

Hall, J. M., & Fields, B. (2012). Race and microaggression in nursing knowledge development. *Advances in Nursing Science, 35*(1), 25-38. https://doi.org/10.1097/ANS.0b013e3182433b70

Halstead, J. & Frank, B. (2017). *Pathways to a nursing Education career: Transitioning from practice to academia* (2nd Ed.). Springer.

Hamzavi, N., & Brown, H. (2023). "Who has been here that looks like me?": A narrative inquiry into Black, Indigenous, and people of color graduate nursing students' experiences of White academic spaces. *Nursing Inquiry, 30*(4), e12568. https://doi.org/10.1111/nin.12568

Hanlon, C. (2022, Mar 12). *Qualtrics: How to add an introduction page to a survey* [Video]. YouTube. https://youtu.be/vLIIwRlR-RA?si=f9xJhj3PvuXjenPk

Harris, C. I. (1995). Whiteness as property. In K. Crenshaw, N. Gotanda, G. Peller, & K. Thomas. (Eds). *Critical race theory: The key writings that formed the movement* (pp. 276-291). The New Press.

Harris, J. (2019). Challenges of nursing faculty retention. *Midwest Quarterly: A Journal of Contemporary Thought, 60*(3), 251-269. https://link.gale.com/apps/doc/A583693211/AONE?u=anon~983f3ef4&sid=googleSchol ar&xid=9824ce5b

Harris, R. C., Rosenberg, L., &. O 'Rourke, M. E. G. (2014). Addressing the challenges of nursing student attrition. *Journal of Nursing Education, 53*(1), 31-37. https://doi.org/10.3928/01484834-20131218-03

Henderson, D., Sewell, K. A., & Wei, H. (2020). The impacts of faculty caring on nursing students' intent to graduate: A systematic literature review. *International journal of nursing sciences, 7*(1), 105-111. https://doi.org/10.1016/j.ijnss.2019.12.009

Hennink, M., & Kaiser, B. N. (2022). Sample sizes for saturation in qualitative research: A systematic review of empirical tests. *Social science & medicine, 292*, 114523. https://doi.org/10.1016/j.socscimed.2021.114523

History.com Editors. (2021 May 24). George Floyd is killed by a police officer, igniting historic protests. *A&E Television Networks.* https://www.history.com/this-day-in-history/george-floyd-killed-by-police-officer

HLS News Staff. (2011, Oct 6). Derrick Bell (1930-2011). *Harvard Law Bulletin* (Winter 2012). https://hls.harvard.edu/today/derrick-bell-1930-2011/

Hoadley-Brill, S. (2024, Jan 15). Martin Luther King, Critical Race Theorist. *The Nation.* https://www.thenation.com/article/society/martin-luther-king-crt/

Hope, A. A., & Munro, C. L. (2023). Through diversity, dignity; through belonging, justice. *American Journal of Critical Care, 32*(6), 397-399. https://doi.org/10.4037/ajcc2023670

Horowitz, J. M. (2019). Most Americans say the legacy of slavery still affects Black people in the U.S. today. *Pew Research Center*. https://www.pewresearch.org/short-reads/2019/06/17/most-americans-say-the-legacy-of-slavery-still-affects-black-people-in-the-u-s-today/

Horsfall, J., Cleary, M., & Hunt, G. E. (2012). Developing a pedagogy for nursing teaching–learning. *Nurse Education Today, 32*(8), 930-933. https://doi.org/10.1016/j.nedt.2011.10.022

Hostetter, M. & Klein, S. (2018, September 17). In focus: Reducing racial disparities in health care by confronting racism. *Transforming Care* [newsletter], Commonwealth Fund. https://www.commonwealthfund.org/publications/2018/sep/focus-reducing-racial-disparities-health-care-confronting-racism

Iheduru-Anderson, K. C., & Alexander, G. R. (2022). Critical race theory: A Framework for the re-education of American nurses. *Creative Nursing, 28*(3), 177-183. https://doi.org/10.1891/CN-2022-0021

Iheduru-Anderson, K. C. & Wahi, M. M. (2022). Race and racism discourse in U.S. nursing: Challenging the silence. *Online Journal of Issues in Nursing*, *27*(1), 1-8. https://doi.org/10.3912/ojin.vol27no01man01

Iheduru-Anderson, K., & Waite, R. (2022). Illuminating antiracist pedagogy in nursing education. *Nursing Inquiry*, *29*(4), e12494. https://doi.org/10.1111/nin.12494

International Council of Nurses (ICN). (n.d.). *Nursing definitions*. https://www.icn.ch/resources/nursing-definitions

Kalb, K. A., O'Conner-Von, S. K., Brockway, C., Rierson, C. L., & Sendelbach, S. (2015). Evidence-based teaching practice in nursing education: Faculty perspectives and practices. *Nursing Education Perspectives (National League for Nursing), 36*(4), 212-

219. https://doi.org/10.5480/14-1472

Kativhu, S. (2021). Covid-19 as a catalyst for digital transformation in higher education: Insights

for rural-based universities in South Africa. *African Renaissance (1744-2532), 18*(4),

285-304. https://hdl.handle.net/10520/ejc-aa_afren_v18_n4_a15

Kavanagh, J. M., & Sharpnack, P. (2021). Crisis in competency: A defining moment in nursing

education. *Online Journal of Issues in Nursing, 26*(1), 1-11.

https://doi.org/10.3912/OJIN.Vol26No01Man02

Kendi, I. X. (2016). *Stamped from the beginning: The definitive history of racist ideas in

America.* Bold Type Books.

Khalifa, M., Dunbar, C., & Douglas, T. (2013). Derrick Bell, CRT, and educational leadership

1995 – present. *Race, Ethnicity and Education, 16*(4), 489-513.

http://dx.doi.org/10.1080/13613324.2013.817770

Kubec, C. (2017). Reducing nursing student attrition: The search for effective

strategies. *Community College Enterprise, 23*(1), 60-68.

https://go.gale.com/ps/i.do?id=GALE%7CA503273284&sid=googleScholar&v=2.1&it=r

&linkaccess=abs&issn=15410935&p=AONE&sw=w&userGroupName=anon%7Ec7f0ec

2c&aty=open-web-entry

Landis, T., Godfrey, N., Barbosa-Leiker, C., Clark, C., Brewington, J., Joseph, M., Luparell, S.,

Phillips, B., Priddy, K., & Weybrew, K. (2022). National study of nursing faculty and

administrators' perceptions of professional identity in nursing. *Nurse Educator, 47*(1), 13-

18. https://doi.org/10.1097/NNE.0000000000001063

Leaver, C. A., Stanley, J. M., & Veenema, T. G. (2022). Impact of the COVID-19 pandemic on

the future of nursing education. *Academic Medicine*, *97*(3), S82.

https://doi.org/10.1097/ACM.0000000000004528

Lewis, N., & Bryan, V. (2021). Andragogy and teaching techniques to enhance adult learners'

experience. *Journal of Nursing Education and Practice, 11*(11), 31-40.

https://doi.org/10.5430/jnep.v11n11p31

Li, L., Wang, Q., & Li, J. (2022). Examining continuance intention of online learning during

COVID-19 pandemic: Incorporating the theory of planned behavior into the expectation–

confirmation model. *Frontiers in Psychology, 13*, 1046407.

https://doi.org/10.3389/fpsyg.2022.1046407

Lincoln, Y. S., Lynham, S. A., & Guba, E. G. (2024). Paradigmatic controversies, contradictions,

and emerging confluences, revisited. In N. K. Denzin, Y. S. Lincoln, M. D. Giardina, &

G. S. Cannella (Eds.), *The SAGE handbook of qualitative research* (6th ed.) (pp. 75-121).

SAGE.

Liu, J. (2023, June 29). The Supreme Court ruled against affirmative action in college

admissions—what students should know. CNBC. *Make It* [newsletter].

https://www.cnbc.com/2023/06/29/scotus-affirmative-action-in-college-admissions-

ruling-what-students-should-know.html

Lopez, V., Anderson J., West, S., & Cleary, M. (2022). Does the COVID-19 pandemic further

impact nursing shortages? *Issues in Mental Health Nursing, 43*(3), 293-295.

https://doi.org/10.1080/01612840.2021.1977875

Louie, P., & Wilkes, R. (2018). Representations of race and skin tone in medical textbook

    imagery. *Social Science & Medicine, 202*, 38–42.

    https://doi.org/10.1016/j.socscimed.2018.02.023

Mariani, B. (2022). The Nursing faculty shortage: It's time to find our voice. *Nursing Education*

    Perspectives, 43(2), 73-73. https://doi.org/10.1097/01.NEP.0000000000000947

Matthews, A. K., Abboud, S., Smith, A. U., Smith, C., Jeremiah, R., Hart, A., & Weaver, T.

    (2022). Strategies to address structural and institutional barriers to success among

    students of color in nursing programs. *Journal of Professional Nursing, 40*, 96-104.

    https://doi.org/10.1016/j.profnurs.2022.03.005

Maxwell, J. A. (2013). *Qualitative research design: An interactive approach.* (3rd ed.). SAGE.

McClain, P. D. (2021). Trump and racial equality in America? No pretense at all! *Policy Studies,*

    42(5/6), 491-508. https://doi.org/10.1080/01442872.2021.1979502

McIntosh, Peggy, & Cleveland, Caitlin. (1990). *White privilege: unpacking the invisible*

    knapsack [Documents]. https://jstor.org/stable/community.30714426

Melnyk, B. M., Fineout-Overholt, E., Stillwell, S. B., & Williamson, K. M. (2009). Igniting a

    spirit of inquiry: An essential foundation for evidence-based practice. *American Journal*

    of Nursing, 109(11), 49-52. DOI: https://doi.org/10.1097/01.NAJ.0000363354.53883.58

Meraji, S. M., Escobar, N., & Devarajan, K., (Hosts). (2020, September 30). Is it time to say

    R.I.P. To 'POC'? [Audio podcast episode]. In *Code Switch.* NPR.

    https://www.npr.org/2020/09/29/918418825/is-it-time-to-say-r-i-p-to-p-o-c

Merriam-Webster Dictionary. (2024). https://www.merriam-webster.com/

Miller, S., & Vaughn, S. (2023). "Everybody's Scrutinizing You": Perspectives of inclusion

among Black and Hispanic nursing students. *Teaching and Learning in Nursing, 18*(1),

98-102. https://doi.org/10.1016/j.teln.2022.09.004

Mills, C. W. (2007). White ignorance. In S. Sullivan & N. Tuana (Eds.), *Race and epistemologies*

of ignorance (pp. 13-38). State University of New York Press.

Mills, C. W. (2022a). Global White ignorance. In *Routledge International Handbook of*

Ignorance Studies (pp. 36-46). Routledge.

http://charleswmills.com/content/Mills_GlobalWhiteIgnorance.pdf

Mills, C. W. (2022b). *The Racial Contract* (Twenty-fifth anniversary edition). Cornell University

Press.

Mitchell, E. A. (2023). Black and African American. *Journal of the Early Republic, 1,* 85-100.

https://doi.org/10.1353/jer.2023.0005

Moore, M. L. (2019). Evidence-based vs. best practice: Here's the difference. *Skin Health*.

https://www.medline.com/strategies/skin-health/evidence-based-vs-best-practice.

Motro, D., Evans, J. B., Ellis, A., & Benson, L. (2022, Jan 31). *The "Angry Black Woman"*

stereotype at work. Harvard Business Review. https://hbr.org/2022/01/the-angry-black-

woman-stereotype-at-work

MSNBC. (2021, June 21). *The ReidOut: Creator of term 'Critical Race Theory' Kimberlé*

Crenshaw explains what it really is [Video]. YouTube.

https://youtu.be/n4TAQF6ocLU?si=e692sfZj8S4z95k8

Murray, T. A., & Noone, J. (2022). Advancing diversity in nursing education: A groundwater

approach. *Journal of Professional Nursing, 41*, 140-148.

https://doi.org/10.1016/j.profnurs.2022.05.002

National Academies of Sciences, Engineering, National Academy of Medicine, Committee on the Future of Nursing, 2020-2030, Flaubert, J. L., Menestrel, S. L., Williams, D. R., & Wakefield, M. K. (2021). *The Future of Nursing 2020-2030: Charting a path to achieve health equity*. National Academies Press. https://nam.edu/publications/the-future-of-nursing-2020-2030/

National Center for Education Statistics. (2023a). *Definitions for new race and ethnicity categories*. Institute of Education Services. https://nces.ed.gov/ipeds/report-your-data/race-ethnicity-definitions

National Center for Education Statistics. (2023b). *Integrated Postsecondary Education Data System (IPEDS)*. Institute of Education Services. https://nces.ed.gov/ipeds/datacenter/InstitutionByName.aspx?goToReportId=6&sid=765d9396-5181-4d87-b383-a7b7a298ad87&rtid=6

National League for Nursing. (2022a). *NLN Faculty census survey of schools of nursing academic year 2020–2021: Executive summary*. https://www.nln.org/docs/default-source/research-statistics/nln-faculty-census-survey-of-schools-of-nursing-academic-year-2020_2022_executive_summary8_29_2022.pdf?sfvrsn=dc89307b_3

National League for Nursing. (2022b). *Research priorities in nursing education*. https://www.nln.org/education/grants-scholarships/research-priorities-in-nursing-education

National Museum of African American History and Culture (NMAAHC). (n.d.). *Talking about race: Whiteness*. Smithsonian. https://nmaahc.si.edu/learn/talking-about-race/topics/Whiteness

Nelson, A. M. (2014). Best practice in nursing: a concept analysis. *International Journal of Nursing Studies, 51*(11), 1507-1516. https://doi.org/10.1016/j.ijnurstu.2014.05.003

Nguyen, M. H., Ramirez, J. J., & Laderman, S. (2023). What counts as a minority-serving institution? Toward the utilization of a standardized and uniform definition and typology. *Educational Researcher, 52*(3), 174-179. https://doi.org/10.3102/0013189X221105861

Nurse-Clarke, N., & Joseph, M. (2022). An exploration of technology acceptance among nursing faculty teaching online for the first time at the onset of the COVID-19 pandemic. *Journal of Professional Nursing, 41*, 8-18. https://doi.org/10.1016/j.profnurs.2022.04.002

Oermann, M. H. (2020). Nursing education research: A new era. *Nurse Educator, 45*(3), 115. https://doi.org/10.1097/NNE.0000000000000830

Office of Management and Budget. (1997, Oct 30). Revisions to the standards for the classification of federal data on race and ethnicity. *Federal Register, 62*(210), 58782-58790. https://www.govinfo.gov/content/pkg/FR-1997-10-30/pdf/97-28653.pdf

Ohito, E. O. (2016). Making the emperor's new clothes visible in anti-racist teacher education: Enacting a pedagogy of discomfort with White preservice teachers. *Equity & Excellence in Education, 49*(4), 454-467. https://doi.org/10.1080/10665684.2016.1226104

Patterson, B. J., & Klein, J. M. (2012). Evidence for teaching: What are faculty using? *Nursing Education Perspectives (National League for Nursing), 33*(4), 240-245. https://doi.org/10.5480/1536-5026-33.4.240

Phillips, J. M., & Malone, B. (2014). Increasing racial/ethnic diversity in nursing to reduce health disparities and achieve health equity. *Public Health Reports, 129*(Suppl. 2), 45–50. https://doi.org/10.1177/00333549141291S209

Pillow, W. (2003). Confession, catharsis, or cure? Rethinking the uses of reflexivity as methodological power in qualitative research. *International journal of qualitative studies in education, 16*(2), 175-196. https://doi.org/10.1080/0951839032000060635

Plano Clark, V. & Creswell, J. W. (2015). *Understanding research: A consumer's guide* (2nd Ed.). Pearson.

Pusey-Reid, E., Gona, C. M., Lussier-Duynstee, P., & Gall, G. (2022). Microaggressions: Black students' experiences. A qualitative study. *Journal of Professional Nursing, 40*, 73-78. https://doi.org/10.1016/j.profnurs.2022.03.004

Pusey-Reid, E., Quinn, L. W., Wong, J., & Wucherpfennig, A. (2023). Representation of dark skin tones in foundational nursing textbooks: an image analysis. *Nurse Education Today, 130*, 105927. https://doi.org/10.1016/j.nedt.2023.105927

Puzan, E. (2003). The unbearable whiteness of being (in nursing). *Nursing Inquiry, 10*(3), 193-200. https://doi.org/10.1046/j.1440-1800.2003.00180.x

Qualtrics. (2023). *Qualtrics XM. Experience management.* https://www.qualtrics.com/

Quaye, S. J., Karikari, S. N., Carter, K. D., Okello, W. K., & Allen, C. (2020). " Why can't I just chill?": The visceral nature of racial battle fatigue. *Journal of College Student Development, 61*(5), 609-623. https://doi.org/10.1353/csd.2020.0058

Ragland Woods, C. C., Chronister, K. M., Perez Grabow, A., Woods, W. E., & Woodlee, K. (2021). Racial battle fatigue: The experiences of Black/African American, biracial Black, and multiracial Black identified graduate students. *Journal of Black Psychology, 47*(4-5), 219-243. https://doi.org/10.1177/00957984211002615

Rankl, F., Johnson, G. A., & Vindrola-Padros, C. (2021). Examining what we know in relation to how we know it: A team-based reflexivity model for rapid qualitative health research.

Qualitative Health Research, 31(7), 1358-1370.

https://doi.org/10.1177/1049732321998062

Rao, B. J. (2019). Innovative teaching pedagogy in nursing education. *International Journal of Nursing Education, 11*(4), 176-180. https://doi.org/10.37506/ijone.v11i4.4040

Redford, P. (2020, Mar 18). *Qualtrics 2: Information and consent* [Video]. YouTube. https://youtu.be/OL0WfAZvVqc?si=gDBTIRP2xpHRfNsC

Rogers, J., Ludwig-Beymer, P., & Baker, M. (2020). Nurse faculty orientation: An integrative review. *Nurse Educator, 45*(6), 343-346. https://doi.org/10.1097/NNE.0000000000000802

Roulston, K. (2024). Examining the "inside lives" of research interviews. In N. K. Denzin, Y. S. Lincoln, M. D. Giardina, & G. S. Cannella (Eds.), *The SAGE handbook of qualitative research* (6th ed., pp. 317-331). SAGE.

Rundell, F. C. (2023). *The art of narrative.* Imagine That Enterprises, LLC.

Saada, J. (2021). Narratives and counter-narratives in law. Uses and critiques of legal narrativism in Critical race theory. *Droit et Société, 108*(2), 319-335. https://doi.org/10.3917/drs1.108.0319

Salisu, W. J., Dehghan Nayeri, N., Yakubu, I., & Ebrahimpour, F. (2019). Challenges and facilitators of professional socialization: A systematic review. *Nursing Open, 6*(4), 1289-1298. https://doi.org./10.1002/nop2.341

Sawyer, L., & Waite, R. (2021). Racial and ethnic diversity in higher education: White privileged resistance and implications for leadership. *Education Policy Analysis Archives, 29*(38). https://doi.org/10.14507/epaa.29.4668

See, E. C. W., Koh, S. S. L., Baladram, S., & Shorey, S. (2023). Role transition of newly graduated nurses from nursing students to registered nurses: A qualitative systematic review. *Nurse Education Today, 121.* https://doi.org/10.1016/j.nedt.2022.105702

Sessler Branden, P., & Sharts-Hopko, N. (2017). Growing clinical and academic nursing leaders: Building the pipeline. *Nursing Administration Quarterly, 41*(3), 258-265. https://doi.org/10.1097/NAQ.0000000000000239

Srikoom, W., Faikhamta, C., & Hanuscin, D. (2018). Dimensions of effective STEM integrated teaching practice. *K-12 STEM Education, 4*(2), 313-330. https://www.learntechlib.org/p/209577/.

Stahl, N. A., & King, J. R. (2020). Understanding and using trustworthiness in qualitative research. *Journal of Developmental Education, 44*(1), 26-28. https://www.jstor.org/stable/45381095

Students for Fair Admissions Inc. v. President and Fellows of Harvard College, 20 U.S. 1199 (2023). https://www.supremecourt.gov/opinions/22pdf/20-1199_hgdj.pdf

Sumpter, D., Thurman, W., Wright, M., Johnson, K., Duplechain, D. & Abbyad, C. (2023). ART Praxis: Evidence-based strategies for antiracist teaching in Nursing. *Nursing Education Perspectives, 44*(5), 273-278. https://doi.org/10.1097/01.NEP.0000000000001171

Tai, D. B., Shah, A., Doubeni, C. A., Sia, I. G., & Wieland, M. L. (2021). The disproportionate impact of COVID-19 on racial and ethnic minorities in the United States, *Clinical Infectious Diseases, 72*(4), 703–706. https://doi.org/10.1093/cid/ciaa815

ten Ham-Baloyi, W., Minnie, K., & van der Walt, C. (2020). Improving healthcare: a guide to roll-out best practices. *African Health Sciences, 20*(3), 1487-1495. https://doi.org/10.4314/ahs.v20i3.55

Thesaurus.com. (2024). *Worry*. https://www.thesaurus.com/browse/worry

Tilki, M., Dye, K., Markey, K., Scholefield, D., Davis, C., & Moore, T. (2007). Racism: The implications for nursing education. *Diversity in Health & Social Care, 4*(4), 303-312. https://www.ana-illinois.org/wp-content/uploads/Racism-the-implications-for-nursing-education.pdf

Tobbell, D. A. (2023). The transformation of American nursing. *Issues in Science and Technology, 39*(3), 74-80. https://issues.org/wp-content/uploads/2023/04/74-80-Tobbell-Transformation-of-American-Nursing-Spring-2023.pdf

Transcultural Nursing Society. (2014). *Standards*. https://tcns.org/standards/

University of North Carolina Asheville. Ramsey Library Video Production. (2015, April 8). *Critical race theory and education: Gloria Ladson-Billings* [Video]. YouTube. https://www.youtube.com/watch?v=katwPTn-nhE

U.S. Bureau of Labor Statistics. (2023 Apr 25). *Occupational employment and wage statistics*. https://www.bls.gov/oes/current/oes291141.htm

U.S. Department of Education, Office of the Under Secretary. (2023, September). *Strategies for increasing diversity and opportunity in higher education.* https://sites.ed.gov/ous/files/2023/09/Diversity-and-Opportunity-in-Higher-Education.pdf

U.S. News & World Report. (2023). *U.S. News education rankings. Colleges.* https://www.usnews.com/best-colleges/rankings

Vagle, M. D., Martin-Kerr, K.G., Miller, J. L., Wald, B., & Fairbanks, H. (2024). Critical post-intentional phenomenological inquiry (CRIT-PIP): Why it matters and what it can do. In N. K. Denzin, Y. S. Lincoln, M. D. Giardina, & G. S. Cannella (Eds.), *The SAGE handbook of qualitative research* (6th ed.) (pp. 223-239). SAGE.

van Manen, M. (2023). *Phenomenology of practice: Meaning-giving methods in phenomenological research and writing*. Taylor & Francis.

van Manen, M., & van Manen, M. (2021). Doing phenomenological research and writing. *Qualitative Health Research, 31*(6), 1069-1082. https://doi.org/10.1177/10497323211003058

Waddell-Henowitch, C. M., Kruth, M. L., & Stephen, H. M. (2022). Reiterating a need for antiracism praxis in nursing and psychiatric nursing education. *The Journal of Nursing Education, 61*(8), 439–446. https://doi.org/10.3928/01484834-20220602-04

Wade, P., Smedley, A., & Takezawa, Y. I. (2024, January 10). Race. *Encyclopedia Britannica*. https://www.britannica.com/topic/race-human

Walters, G., Hoffart, N., Kring, D., Whitley, T., Horne, L., & Almotairy, M. (2022). Work readiness of newly licensed RNs. *JONA: The Journal of Nursing Administration, 52*(9), 469-473. https://doi.org/10.1097/NNA.0000000000001184

Weberg, D., Chan, G., & Dicków, M. (2021). Disrupting nursing education in light of COVID-19. *Online Journal of Issues in Nursing, 26*(1), 1-9. https://doi.org/10.3912/OJIN.Vol26No01Man04

Wesp, L. M., Scheer, V., Ruiz, A., Walker, K., Weitzel, J., Shaw, L., Kako, P. M., & Mkandawire-Valhmu, L. (2018). An emancipatory approach to cultural competency: The application of critical race, postcolonial, and intersectionality theories. *Advances in Nursing Science, 41*(4), 316-326. https://doi.org/10.1097/ANS.0000000000000230

West, C. (1995). Foreword. In K. Crenshaw, N. Gotanda, G. Peller, & K. Thomas (Eds.), *Critical race theory: The key writings that formed the movement* (pp. xi-xii). The New Press.

White, B. J., & Fulton, J. S. (2015). Common experiences of African American nursing students:

An integrative review. *Nursing Education Perspectives, 36*(3), 167-175.

https://doi.org/10.5480/14-1456

White, B. J., Mentag, N. M., & Kaunda, B. R. (2020). African American nurses describe

experiences of mistrust and trust while in nursing school. *Nursing Education

Perspectives, 41*(3), 157-162. https://doi.org/10.1097/01.NEP.0000000000000606

World Health Organization. (2023). *Nursing and midwifery. Overview.*

https://www.who.int/health-topics/nursing#tab=tab_1

Wray, J., Aspland, J., Barrett, D., & Gardiner, E. (2017). Factors affecting the program

completion of pre-registration nursing students through a three-year course: A

retrospective cohort study. *Nurse Education in Practice, 24,* 14–20.

https://doi.org/10.1016/j.nepr.2017.03.002

Yordy, K. D. (2006). *The nursing faculty shortage: A crisis for health care.*

Association of Academic Health Centers.

https://folio.iupui.edu/bitstream/handle/10244/533/NursingFacultyShortage071006.pdf

Zoom. (2024). *Support. What is Zoom video conferencing?*

https://support.zoom.com/hc/en/article?id=zm_kb&sysparm_article=KB0059590

Appendix A: Consent To Participate in Research Interview

Meanings of the Phenomenon of Racism for Nursing Educators at Predominately White Institutions (PWIs)

LeRai Martin
Doctoral Candidate
Educational Policy and Strategic Leadership Department
in the School of Business, Education & Professional Studies
at Cabrini University
Email for primary author—LM7013@Cabrini.edu

This study involves your participation in research. The purpose of the research is to explore meanings of the phenomenon of racism for nursing faculty, staff, and administrators at Predominately White Institutions' (PWIs) and their understanding of the significance of the experience of racism for Black nursing students. Sensitive material may include an emotional or similar risk. Participants may feel anxious recalling and discussing experiences related to race and racism. If you feel more anxious or upset, you may contact the National Mental Health Crisis Line by calling or texting 988. Benefits of participation in this study include learning more about the phenomenon of racism in nursing and the effects on Black students. However, most protocols will not benefit individual participants. The research data is being used for a dissertation study the doctoral candidate is completing at Cabrini University. The findings of this study will be included as part of the researcher's dissertation defense and published dissertation. The findings will also be presented at a student research symposium at Cabrini University and may be submitted for subsequent publication in a peer-reviewed academic journal.

The participant will be asked to participate in an individual interview with the researcher via Zoom. This study also includes a separate online qualitative survey. Participants in the interview may opt to complete the survey, but survey completion is not required for participation in the interview. Participants will be selected from among individuals currently employed as nursing faculty, staff, and/or administrators at Predominately White Institutions. Predominately White Institutions are colleges & universities in which White students comprise at least half (50%) of the student population. At the beginning of the interview, the researcher will ask approximately 14 demographic questions. Then the researcher will ask 11 open-ended questions to learn about the participant's experience with racism, definitions of racism, and understanding of the challenges of racism for Black nursing students. Total time to review the consent form and complete the interview is anticipated to be 30 - 45 minutes. Your participation will take approximately 45 minutes total. The interview will be audio and video recorded through the Zoom application.

All information will be kept confidential which means that no one can access the data except the primary researcher and faculty mentor. "Confidential" means steps are taken to protect the participants' identity, personal and private information from being revealed to anyone except the researcher and faculty mentor. Only aggregate data will be analyzed.

Research data involving interviews cannot be anonymous which means that it may be possible to determine the identity of the participant. No personal identifying information will be used in any research results/publication.

Remember your participation is voluntary, and you may stop participation at any time. There is no penalty for not participating or withdrawing from the research study. You will not be penalized if you choose not to answer a demographic question due to its sensitive nature. There is no compensation for participation. The alternative to participating is not to participate. Participant's consent is required to participate in the interview. The participant is not required to agree to audio/video recording to participate in the interview. The recording options are audio only, audio and video recording, or no recording.

Please contact the primary researcher with any questions, concerns, or complaints about the research and any research-related injuries by e-mailing LM7013@Cabrini.edu or the Chair of the Institutional Review Board at irb@cabrini.edu. This research has been reviewed and approved by Cabrini University's Institutional Review Board (IRB). The approved IRB protocol number for this study is #EDD 24-27.

Research data retention protocol: Transcripts from interviews and survey data will be kept for one year, or until the researcher has completed the doctoral program at Cabrini University and subsequent publication for a peer-reviewed journal. Video and audio recordings will be permanently deleted by the researcher after the researcher has extracted data from those sources. The researcher expects to complete data extraction and deletion of video and audio tapes by May 1, 2024. Research data will be kept on a computer hard drive, secured by a password only known to the researcher. This data will be destroyed by permanently deleting it from the hard drive at the end of the aforementioned time period.

By signing the following, you give your consent for the primary researcher listed above to use your data in this study. If you wish to withdraw from this study at any time, simply communicate this to the researcher and your data will be destroyed. * Please indicate if you are willing to have this interview recorded. You may still participate in this study even if you do not want the interview recorded.

I agree to audio/video recording in this study _____

I agree to audio recording only in this study _____

I do not agree to audio/video recording in this study _____

Print Name ____

Sign Name ____

Date ___________________________________

Meanings of the Phenomenon of Racism for Nursing Educators at Predominately White Institutions (PWIs)
LeRai Carter Martin
Department of Education, Cabrini University
Email for primary author—LM7013@Cabrini.edu

Please contact the primary researcher any with questions, concerns, or complaints about the research and any research-related injuries by e-mailing LM7013@cabrini.edu or the Chair of the Institutional Review Board at irb@cabrini.edu. This research has been reviewed and approved by Cabrini University's Institutional Review Board (IRB). The approved IRB protocol number for this study is EDD 24-27. Sensitive material may include an emotional or similar risk. The research involves questions that may provoke anxiety. Participants may feel more anxious following the completion of this survey. If you feel more anxious or upset, you may contact the National Mental Health Crisis Line by calling or texting 988.

LeRai Carter Martin   *February 15, 2024*
Primary Researcher Signature   Date

Appendix B: Consent To Participate in Research Survey

Meanings of the Phenomenon of Racism for Nursing Educators at Predominately White Institutions (PWIs)

LeRai Martin
Doctoral Candidate
Educational Policy and Strategic Leadership Department
in the School of Business, Education & Professional Studies
at Cabrini University
Email for primary author—LM7013@Cabrini.edu

This study involves your participation in research. The purpose of the research is to explore meanings of the phenomenon of racism for nursing faculty, staff, and administrators at Predominately White Institutions' (PWIs) and their understanding of the significance of the experience of racism for Black nursing students. Sensitive material may include an emotional or similar risk. Participants may feel anxious recalling and discussing experiences related to race and racism. If you feel more anxious or upset, you may contact the National Mental Health Crisis Line by calling or texting 988. Benefits of participation in this study include learning more about the phenomenon of racism in nursing and the effects on Black students. However, most protocols will not benefit individual participants. The research data is being used for a dissertation study the doctoral candidate is completing at Cabrini University. The findings of this study will be included as part of the researcher's dissertation defense and published dissertation. The findings will also be presented at a student research symposium at Cabrini University and may be submitted for subsequent publication in a peer-reviewed academic journal.

The participant will be asked to participate in an online qualitative survey via Qualtrics. This study also includes a separate individual interview with the researcher. Participants in the survey may opt to participate in the interview, but interview completion is not required for participation in the survey. Participants will be selected from among individuals currently employed as nursing faculty, staff, and/or administrators at Predominately White Institutions. Predominately White Institutions are colleges & universities in which White students comprise at least half (50%) of the student population. Participants will be asked to select or type their answers to 11-15 demographic questions and type their responses to 7 open-ended questions. The purpose of the survey is to learn about the participant's experience with racism, definitions of racism, and understanding of the challenges of racism for Black nursing students. Total time to review the consent form and complete the survey is anticipated to be 15 - 20 minutes. Your participation will take approximately 15-20 minutes total.

All information will be kept confidential which means that no one can access the data except the primary researcher and faculty mentor. "Confidential" means steps are taken to protect the participants' identity, personal and private information from being revealed to anyone except the researcher and faculty mentor. Only aggregate data will be analyzed.

Research data will be anonymous. Anonymous means that research data cannot be traced to the individual participant. No personal identifying information will be used in any research results/publication.

Remember your participation is voluntary, and you may stop participation at any time. There is no penalty for not participating or withdrawing from the research study. You will not be penalized if you choose not to answer a question due to its sensitive nature. There is no compensation for participation. The alternative to participating is not to participate. Participant's consent is required to participate in the survey.

Please contact the primary researcher with any questions, concerns, or complaints about the research and any research-related injuries by e-mailing LM7013@Cabrini.edu or the Chair of the Institutional Review Board at irb@cabrini.edu. This research has been reviewed and approved by Cabrini University's Institutional Review Board (IRB). The approved IRB protocol number for this study is #EDD 24-27.

Research data retention protocol: Survey data will be kept for one year, or until the researcher has completed the doctoral program at Cabrini University and subsequent publication for a peer-reviewed journal. Research data will be kept on a computer hard drive, secured by a password only known to the researcher. This data will be destroyed by permanently deleting it from the hard drive at the end of the aforementioned time period.

By clicking on the NEXT button, you give your consent for the primary researcher listed above to use your data in this study. If you wish to withdraw from this study at any time, simply close out the online portal/website to discontinue your participation at this time.

Appendix C: Data Collection Instrument: Online Qualitative Survey of Nursing Educators

LeRai Martin
Doctoral Candidate
Educational Policy and Strategic Leadership Department
in the School of Business, Education & Professional Studies
at Cabrini University
Email for primary author—LM7013@Cabrini.edu

Introduction to the Study:

My name is LeRai Martin, RN, MSN. I am an EdD candidate in the Higher Education Leadership program at Cabrini University. I am conducting research to explore meanings of the phenomenon of racism and the effects of racism on Black nursing students for nursing educators at Predominately White Institutions (PWIs).

Your contribution to this study will add richness and depth to what is already known about nursing faculty, staff, administrators. Please share your unique voice and valuable experiences by completing this online qualitative survey. The survey is confidential and your responses are anonymous. Anonymous means that research data cannot be traced to the individual participant.

You will be asked to type your responses to 7 open-ended questions and answer approximately 15 demographic questions. Overall, the estimated response time for the survey is approximately 15-20 minutes. You may take as little or as much time as you would like responding to the survey.

I hope you feel comfortable with typing your responses to a few questions about the topic of racism and nursing education. Racism is a sensitive topic and discussing it may involve an emotional or similar risk. If you feel distressed by this survey, please contact the Crisis Lifeline for support. Thank you for choosing to share today. Your time is precious and your participation is appreciated.

☐ By checking this box, you give your consent to participate in this study.

Demographics:

1. Do you work as faculty, staff, or an administrator in a <u>pre-licensure</u>, <u>undergraduate</u> nursing program at a Predominately White Institution (PWI)? A PWI is a college or university where at least half of the enrolled students are White.

A. Yes

B. No

If "Yes", proceed with demographic questions & interview. If "No", discontinue interview and thank the respondent for their time and interest.

2. What is your role?

A. Faculty

B. Staff

    C. Administrator

    D. Other. Please name your role________________________________

3. Please describe your role _______________________________

4. Which of the following types of Nursing programs do you SUPPORT/ADMINISTER/TEACH? (Select all that apply)

    A. 4-year baccalaureate degree (RN) – pre-licensure

    B. Accelerated BSN program – pre-licensure

    C. Direct-entry master's degree (RN) – pre-licensure

    D. RN-to-BSN program

    E. 2-year associate degree (RN)

    F. Diploma (RN)

    G. Licensed practical nursing certificate (LPN)

    H. Other, please specify ___________________

5. What is your schedule type?

    A. Full-time

    B. Part-time

    C. Adjunct

    D. Visiting lecturer/other

    E. Prefer not to say

6. How many years have you worked in this specific position?

7. How many years have you worked in nursing education?

8. What is the highest degree or level of education you have completed?

    A. High School

    B. Vocational/Technical School

    C. Associate's Degree

    D. Bachelor's Degree

    E. Master's Degree

    F. Terminal degree – Please specify type (PhD, EdD, DNP...) ___________

    G. Post-doctoral studies

    H. Prefer not to say

FACULTY ONLY (questions 9-12):

9. Do you currently teach, or have you ever taught, in the classroom/didactic setting?

    A. Yes

    B. No

    9a. If YES to 9, was/is your classroom/didactic course conducted primarily in-person, online, or in a hybrid format?

    A. In-person
    B. Online
    C. Hybrid

10. Do you currently teach, or have you ever taught, in the clinical or laboratory setting?
    A. Yes
    B. No

      10a. If YES to 10, was/is your clinical/laboratory course conducted primarily in-person, online, or in a hybrid format?
      A. In-person
      B. Online
      C. Hybrid

11. Does your institution have a tenure system?
    A. Yes
    B. No

      11a. If "Yes", what is your tenure status at your institution?
      A. Tenured
      B. Tenure-track
      C. Continuing Non-Tenured
      D. Adjunct/Part-time
      E. Prefer not to say

12. What is your rank/professional level at your institution?
    A. Professor
    B. Associate Professor
    C. Assistant Professor
    D. Other. Please specify ______________________
    E. Prefer not to say

13. What is your age?

14. What is your gender?

15. What is your race/ethnicity?

Open-ended Survey Questions

1. Please describe the cultural, racial, ethnic diversity of the students, faculty and staff of your nursing program.

2. How would you describe racism in general? Sometimes it is easier to use metaphor or imagery to describe a phenomenon (a thing). For example, one might say that racism smells like…, or racism reminds them of… Feel free to be creative.

3. Have you witnessed any situations in nursing education that you would describe as being racist or discriminatory towards another person? If so, please describe the incident.

4. What are some of the challenges you think Black students might face in your nursing education program?

5. How do faculty, staff, and administrators address racism in nursing education?

6. Please share the support systems in place for Black students in your nursing program.

7. Please add anything else you would like to discuss about your knowledge and experience of racism in your work in nursing education.

Thank you for your participation in this study. Your responses are anonymous and will be kept confidential. Only aggregate data will be analyzed. Research data will be obtained for up to one year after the study. Research data will be stored on the primary researcher's password-secured harddrive and destroyed upon publication or within one year of this study.

Please contact the primary researcher at with any questions, concerns, or complaints about the research and any research-related injuries by emailing lm7013@cabrini.edu or the Chair of the Institutional Review Board at irb@cabrini.edu. This study has been reviewed and approved by Cabrini University's Institutional Review Board (IRB). The approved IRB number for this study is EDD 24-27

Appendix D: Data Collection Instrument: Interview Protocol: Faculty
LeRai Martin
Doctoral Candidate
Educational Policy and Strategic Leadership Department
in the School of Business, Education & Professional Studies
at Cabrini University

Meanings of the Phenomenon of Racism for Nursing Educators at Predominately White Institutions

Please note: This protocol will be used to guide the interview process. The participant will not have access to this protocol. Individuals working in multiple roles (e.g., faculty & admin) will be asked to select one role to represent for this study.

Opening Script

Thank you for choosing to share today. Your voice and your experiences are valuable. What you share in today's interview will add richness and depth to what we know, *how* we know, and how we do things in nursing education. I hope you feel comfortable sharing with me today. Your responses in this interview are confidential. I will ask you a few questions that require you to think about and respond to what may be a difficult topic to discuss. This study is about the *Meanings of the Phenomenon of Racism for Nursing Educators at Predominately White Institutions*. I want to hear your thoughts, opinions, and feelings about racism and nursing education. We will begin with a few demographic questions:

Demographic Questions

1. Do you work as FACULTY in a <u>pre-licensure</u>, <u>undergraduate</u> nursing program at a Predominately White Institution (PWI)? A PWI is a college or university where at least half of the enrolled students are White.

  A. Yes
  B. No

If "Yes", proceed with demographic questions & interview. If "No", discontinue interview and thank the respondent for their time.

2. Please describe your role _______________________________________

3. What is your AGE?

4. What is your GENDER?

5. What is your RACE/ETHNICITY?

6. What is the HIGHEST DEGREE or level of education you have completed?

7. In which of the following types of Nursing programs do you TEACH? (Select all that apply.)
    A. 4-year baccalaureate degree (RN) – pre-licensure
    B. Accelerated BSN program – pre-licensure
    C. Direct-entry master's degree (RN) – pre-licensure
    D. RN-to-BSN program
    E. 2-year associate degree (RN)
    F. Diploma (RN)
    G. Licensed practical nursing certificate (LPN)
    H. Other, please specify ___________________

8. What is your schedule type?
    A. Full-time
    B. Part time
    C. Adjunct
    D. Visiting lecturer/other
    E. Prefer not to say

9. How many years have you worked in this specific position?

10. How many years have you worked in nursing education?

11. Do you currently teach, or have you ever taught, in the classroom/didactic setting?
    A. Yes
    B. No

    11a. If YES to 11, was/is your classroom/didactic course conducted primarily in-person, online, or in a hybrid format?
    A. In-person
    B. Online
    C. Hybrid

12. Do you currently teach, or have you ever taught, in the clinical/laboratory setting?
    A. Yes
    B. No

    12a. If YES to 12, was/is your clinical/laboratory course conducted primarily in-person, online, or in a hybrid format?
    A. In-person
    B. Online
    C. Hybrid

13. What is your rank/professional level at your institution?

A. Professor
B. Associate Professor
C. Assistant Professor
D. Other. Please specify _______________________
E. Prefer not to say

14. Does your institution have a tenure system?
A. Yes
B. No

    14a. If "Yes", what is your tenure status at your institution?
    A. Tenured
    B. Tenure-track
    C. Continuing Non-Tenured
    D. Adjunct/Part-time
    E. Prefer not to say

Open-ended Interview Questions

(Warm up questions)
1. What do you like best about working in nursing education?

2. What do you like best about the curriculum of the nursing program where you teach (answer for the program in which you teach most of your courses, if teaching in multiple programs)? ▢

(Script): Let's talk a little about working in a culturally diverse environment:
3. How does teaching students from different cultural/racial/ethnic backgrounds influence your instructional practices? *(Follow up. Be inquisitive, ask for an example to illustrate the response).*

(Script): Let's talk a little about race and racism in general. This is a sensitive topic. I appreciate your willingness to share your thoughts, feelings, and experiences with racism and nursing education. I will ask you a few questions that require you to think about and respond to what may be a difficult topic to discuss:

4. What experiences with (or exposure to) racism or discrimination against another person have you had?

(Prompt question): ***4a.*** Have you witnessed any situations or incidences that you would describe as being racist or discriminatory towards another person? ***4b.*** If so, please describe the experience.

5. How would you define racism?

(Prompt question): ***5a.*** Sometimes it is easier to use metaphor or imagery(?) to describe a phenomenon (a thing). For example, one might say that racism smells like…, or racism reminds them of… Feel free to be creative

6. Do you think about racism in your everyday work?

***If yes,* please elaborate.**

(Script): Let's talk a little about race and racism in nursing education.

7. What are your personal experiences with racism in nursing education?

(Prompt question): ***7a.*** Have you witnessed any situations or incidences that you would describe as being racist or discriminatory towards another person? ***7b.*** If so, please describe the experience.

(Script): Now, let's talk a little about nursing students. Peer-reviewed journal articles that focused on the lived experience of students of color in nursing school have reported that Black students have described being excluded and feeling isolated in nursing educational settings.

8. What do you think about this? (the research findings that were just read)?

9. How engaged are Black students in the classes you teach compared to other students?

10. What are some of the challenges you think Black students might face in your nursing education program?

If they mention YES there are challenges in the previous question, ask

10a. What are some of the ways that you think you can support Black students in your nursing program?

□

If they say there are NO challenges in the previous question, say □
10b. It is wonderful that there are no challenges for Black students in your program. Please tell me about the support systems in place for Black students in your nursing program?

11. Please add anything else you would like to discuss about this topic.

(Script): Your time is precious and I respect it. Thank you very much for your participation in this study.

I am including my email in the chat. (Type it in)
My email is also accessible in the invitation you received to participate in the study. Please email me if you have any questions or concerns about today's interview. I will be in touch with a copy of the recording/transcript for your review.

Appendix E: Data Collection Instrument: Interview Protocol: Staff

LeRai Martin
Doctoral Candidate
Educational Policy and Strategic Leadership Department
in the School of Business, Education & Professional Studies
at Cabrini University

Meanings of the Phenomenon of Racism for Nursing Educators at Predominately White Institutions

Please note: This protocol will be used to guide the interview process. The participant will not have access to this protocol. Individuals working in multiple roles (e.g., faculty & admin) will be asked to select one role to represent for this study.

Opening Script

Thank you for choosing to share today. Your voice and your experiences are valuable. What you share in today's interview will add richness and depth to what we know, *how* we know, and how we do things in nursing education. I hope you feel comfortable sharing with me today. Your responses in this interview are confidential. I will ask you a few questions that require you to think about and respond to what may be a difficult topic to discuss. This study is about the *Meanings of the Phenomenon of Racism for Nursing Educators at Predominately White Institutions*. I want to hear your thoughts, opinions, and feelings about racism and nursing education. We will begin with a few demographic questions:

Demographic Questions

1. Do you work as STAFF in a <u>pre-licensure</u>, <u>undergraduate</u> nursing program at a Predominately White Institution (PWI)? A PWI is a college or university where at least half of the enrolled students are White.

    A. Yes
    B. No

If "Yes", proceed with demographic questions & interview. If "No", discontinue interview and thank the respondent for their time.

2. Please describe your role ___________________________________

3. What is your AGE?

4. What is your GENDER?

5. What is your RACE OR ETHNICITY?

6. What is the HIGHEST DEGREE or level of education you have completed?

7. Which of the following types of Nursing programs do you SUPPORT? (Select all that apply)
   A. 4-year baccalaureate degree (RN) – pre-licensure
   B. Accelerated BSN program – pre-licensure
   C. Direct-entry master's degree (RN) – pre-licensure
   D. RN-to-BSN program
   E. 2-year associate degree (RN)
   F. Diploma (RN)
   G. Licensed practical nursing certificate (LPN)
   H. Other, please specify ___________________

8. What is your schedule type?
   A. Full-time
   B. Part time
   C. Adjunct
   D. Visiting lecturer/other
   E. Prefer not to say

9. How many years have you worked in this specific position?

10. How many years have you worked in nursing education?

Open-ended Interview Questions

(Warm up questions)
1. What do you like best about working in nursing education?

2. What do you like best about working with nursing students/faculty?

(Script): Let's talk a little about working in a culturally diverse environment.

3. How does working with or around individuals from different cultural/racial/ethnic backgrounds influence your work?

(Script): Let's talk a little about race and racism in general. This is a sensitive topic. I appreciate your willingness to share your thoughts, feelings, and experiences with racism and nursing education. I will ask you a few questions that require you to think about and respond to what may be a difficult topic to discuss:

4. What experiences with (or exposure to) racism or discrimination against another person have you had?

> *Prompt question: **4a**. Have you witnessed any situations or incidences that you would describe as being racist or discriminatory towards another person? **4b**. If so, please describe the experience.*

5. How would you define racism?

> *Prompt question: **5a**. Sometimes it is easier to use metaphor or imagery(?) to describe a phenomenon (a thing). For example, one might say that racism smells like…, or racism reminds them of… Feel free to be creative*

6. Do you think about racism in your everyday work?

> *If* yes, **please elaborate.**

(Script): Let's talk a little about race and racism in nursing education.

7. What are your personal experiences with racism in nursing education?

> *(Prompt question):* **7a.** Have you witnessed any situations or incidences that you would describe as being racist or discriminatory towards another person? **7b.** If so, please describe the experience.

Now, let's talk a little about nursing students. Peer-reviewed journal articles that focused on the lived experience of students of color in nursing school have reported that Black students have described being excluded and feeling isolated in nursing educational settings.

8. What do you think about this? (the research findings that were just read)?